The Canterbury Tales

Forth we rode when day began to spring

THE
CANTERBURY TALES

OF

GEOFFREY CHAUCER

A MODERN RENDERING INTO PROSE OF
THE PROLOGUE AND NINE TALES
BY
PERCY MACKAYE

WITH PICTURES IN COLOR BY
WALTER APPLETON CLARK

AVENEL BOOKS
NEW YORK

Originally published as
The Canterbury Tales of Geoffrey Chaucer.

Published in 1987 by Avenel Books, distributed by Crown Publishers, Inc.,
225 Park Avenue South, New York, New York 10003.

Printed and bound in the United States of America

Library of Congress Cataloging-in-Publication Data

MacKaye, Percy, 1875–1956.
    The Canterbury tales of Geoffrey Chaucer.

    I. Chaucer, Geoffrey, d. 1400. Canterbury tales.
Selections.   II. Title.
PR1872.M3   1987   821'.1   87–19324
ISBN 0-517-63206-3

h g f e d c b a

Contents

		Page
List of Color Illustrations	. . . .	vii
About This Illustrated Edition	. . . .	ix
Foreword	. . . .	xi
Glossary of Unfamiliar Words	. . . .	xv
Preface to the First Edition	. . . .	xxi
The Prologue	. . . .	7
The Knight's Tale	. . . .	26
The Prologue of the Nun's Priest's Tale	. . . . . .	74
The Nun's Priest's Tale	. . . .	76
Epilogue to the Nun's Priest's Tale	. . . . . .	91
The Physician's Tale	. . . .	92
Words of the Host	. . . .	99
The Prologue of the Pardoner's Tale	. . . . . .	101
The Pardoner's Tale	. . . .	104

CONTENTS

		Page
The Wife of Bath's Prologue	. . . .	116
The Tale of the Wife of Bath	. . . .	134
The Clerk's Prologue	. . . .	144
The Clerk's Tale	. . . .	146
The Squire's Tale	. . . .	173
The Words of the Franklin	. . . .	188
The Franklin's Prologue	. . . .	189
The Franklin's Tale	. . . .	189
The Canon's Yeoman's Prologue	. . . .	210
The Canon's Yeoman's Tale	. . . .	214
Notes	. . . .	231

Illustrations in Color

Forth we rode when the day began to spring . . . . . *Frontispiece*

Facing
page

Therewith he brought us out of Town 16

Palamon desireth to slay his foe Arcite 48

The three Rogues search in the woods for Death 80

So much of Dalliance and fair Speech 144

There came a Knight upon a Steed of Brass 176

About this Illustrated Edition

This rare and long-forgotten edition of *The Canterbury Tales* is graced with the original illustrations of Walter Appleton Clark, commissioned for the first edition of this book early in this century. Their striking stained-glass quality is highly appropriate for their subject matter—a religious pilgrimage—while their vigor and color reflect a Chaucerian zest for life.

Walter Appleton Clark was a gifted painter and illustrator, noted for his richly imaginative art which combined delicacy and strength. Clark was a short-lived genius who died at thirty. Coming from a family that traced its roots back to Charlemagne, he may well have felt a special affinity for these ancient scenes; we do know that he considered them his most important work. The publishers of this Avenel edition can only agree, and are proud to reprint this gem of the past.

CLAIRE BOOSS
EDITOR

1987

Acknowledgment

The publisher would like to thank Ann Miller for her contributions in creating the glossary and providing translations and footnotes to this edition.

Foreword

Prepare for a journey through an ancient land, fourteenth-century England, where quiet dirt roads wind through the virgin forest, and robbers lie in waiting; where fires crackle throughout the night in taverns and inns that give comfort to the weary traveler who stops to rest. It is a time of cold, clean, spring mornings when the hot breath of horses steams before their noses, and the evening shadows cast by candle, lamp, and moonlight contain the mysteries and visions of medieval people steeped in superstition and an early Christianity that predates Shakespeare by three hundred years.

We join a pilgrimage to Canterbury, to the shrine of Saint Thomas à Becket, who was canonized less than two centuries before. We want to stand before the remains of a man who opposed a king who put himself before God, was murdered for it, and came to be the most blessed figure in his homeland. In days when news travels slowly and passage is arduous and fraught with danger, everyone knows of his martyrdom, and they come from city and hamlet, country cottage and cavernous castle to kneel in homage to his enormous display of principle. Had he not been chancellor of England and archbishop of Canterbury? Had he not known the security of friendship with his ruler, Henry II? And had he not forsaken it all because that ruler tried to curtail the power of his church, the one church of which he, Becket, was an official representative? Yes, he is much loved and much honored. Common men and great lords call on him for aid in sickness and misfortune. He is held high as an example of courage and perseverance.

And what of the poet whose words transcend the centuries and enable us to walk beside the horses of these wayfarers in their nuns' habits, their priests' robes, and the brightly colored raiment of a diverse laity? What of Geoffrey Chaucer, this genius who has given us a glimpse not only of a great language being born, but also of the lives and

FOREWORD

legends of his fellow men, with whom he broke bread and drank wine? We know that at age eight or nine, he survived the plague of 1349, known as the Black Death, that killed one quarter of the population of Europe. We know that as a young man he fought in the Hundred Years War, in 1359–60, for Edward III and John the Gaunt, then a very influential man at court. In 1367, he married the sister of Katherine Roet who later married John the Gaunt. John and Katherine's son was to become Henry IV in 1399, a year before Chaucer's death. These powerful connections were no doubt at least partially responsible for Chaucer's activities in government. He was sent on several diplomatic missions to the Continent (1370–78), and he made three visits to Italy. He held important official positions, and in 1386 he sat in Parliament at Westminster as knight for the Shire of Kent. He was indeed a worldly fellow, and the world to which he has given us entry was certainly no stranger to him. He was not an artist in an ivory tower who cast his works down to an esthetically impoverished populace.

The journey proceeds at a leisurely pace. (Speed over a long distance is unthinkable.) For reasons that will be made clear in the Prologue, each member of our band is encouraged to tell a story. We should keep reminding ourselves that these are religious men and women anticipating a visit to their patron saint's burial ground. Their tales are, therefore, mainly of a moral nature, and herein lies a lesson that has been passed down to us. We hear of love, jealousy, brotherhood, faith, motherhood, marriage, deceit, greed, and betrayal. We reflect that, although the world has changed dramatically, human nature has remained somewhat the same. While today, in our technologically advanced, fast-paced world, we might view moral issues as more subjective than did Chaucer's pilgrims, we still suffer from and delight in the same feelings and states of being as they did. But there is a major difference in our modern life that we note in reading these accounts, and little by little, it becomes clear. One ingredient in *The Canterbury Tales* is missing today: the miracles. There are no more miracles. At first, this is the saddest of all realizations, and then a corresponding fact softens the blow. As there are no miracles, neither are there inquisitions, burning at the stake, trials of witches, or devils in the moonlight. Religious persecution, where it exists—and it still does—is considered evil by rational people everywhere. It would be wonderful to witness a miracle, but if such a phenomenon is not possible without the corresponding horror, we are, no doubt, better off without it.

xii

FOREWORD

But, returning to the voyage at hand—roll up your sleeping bag, make sure you've got a good strong pair of walking shoes, and bring a variety of clothing for changes in the weather. We're off to visit St. Thomas at Canterbury, and who knows whom we'll meet along the way.

KENNETH H. BROWN

New York City
1987

Glossary of Unfamiliar Words

Reader should also refer to Notes at back of book

affray	frighten
anon	at once
assoil	absolve, pardon
astonied	amazed
baldric	strap worn over the shoulder and across the chest to support sword or bugle
benefice	financial support from a church
bream and luce	two popular varieties of freshwater fish
caitiff	captive, wretch
caul	hairnet
chamberlain	person responsible for the management of a chamber/chambers
chantry	payment for masses
chough	crow (see Note to p. 120)
churl	ruffian
cinque	five
clout	rag

GLOSSARY OF UNFAMILIAR WORDS

consistory	court of justice
cozen	deceive, outsmart
crupper	horse's hindquarters
devoir	duty
eke	moreover
electuary	medicine
endite	write, compose
ensample	example
espy	watch; discover
explicit	he explains
fee simple	unrestricted possession
franklin	country gentleman
fustian	a thick, coarse cotton cloth
gan espy	watched
gin	device, trap
gossip	close friend
guerdon	reward
habergeon	coat of mail
hart	deer

GLOSSARY OF UNFAMILIAR WORDS

hauberk	a sleeveless coat of mail
hazardry	gambling
holt	woodland
horologe	clock
husbandry	tending, managing
jupon	tunic
justice in assize	circuit judge
kine	cows
kirtle	long gown
kite	a predatory bird
latten	copper and zinc compound; brass
laud	praise
leech	doctor
licentiate	licensed confessor
liefer	rather
limiter	a friar licensed to seek revenues within a limited area
list	wish, desire; *I list full ill to sport,* I have no desire to jest
lists	enclosure, arena for formal knightly combat
lusty	pleasant

GLOSSARY OF UNFAMILIAR WORDS

malisoun	curse
manciple	a purchaser of provisions for an institution such as a college
maugre	in spite of
mead	meadow
mew	pen, coop
mickle	much
motley	a cloth woven of several colors
niggard	miser
paid of	satisfied with
philosopher	an alchemist
physic	medicine
pies	magpies (noisy birds)
plaintain and pellitory	herbs
point-device	exactly
poitrel	horse's collar
pricked	spurred
privy	private, secret
provost	magistrate
quit	repay, reward; *quit you your guerdon*, give you your reward

GLOSSARY OF UNFAMILIAR WORDS

reck	reach
rede	advice
reeve	an overseer chosen from among a manor's serfs to collect rents, maintain order
ruth	pity, sorrow
sarcenet	a fine silk cloth
semicope	short cape
shriven	absolved
smite; smote	strike; struck
sooth	truth, true, truly
sop	toasted bread or cake
stews	brothels
stint	cease
summoner	an official—often corrupt, and much hated—who summoned sinners to appear before the ecclesiastical court, which took particular notice of sexual immorality
targe	shield
tercelet	male falcon
thrall	slave
tippet	cape
trey	three

GLOSSARY OF UNFAMILIAR WORDS

trow (trowed)	suppose(d), believe(d)
tun	cask
victuallers	suppliers of victuals, i.e., food and drink
wax	become
weal	good fortune, wellbeing
ween	believe
whilom	once, in the past
wight	person, creature
wist	knew
wont; wonted	custom; customary
worship	dignity, appearance
wot	know
wroth	angry
yeoman	an attendant
Zephirus	the west wind

Preface to the First Edition

THE barrier of obsolete speech is the occasion and the apology for this rendering of the Canterbury Tales in English easily intelligible to-day. Whether this barrier be real, or but generally assumed, matters little, for the assumption itself is obstructive and tends equally to the resultant fact, that—in spite of the immensely widened interest in Chaucer and the diffused knowledge of his works due to labours of profound scholarship in the last fifty years—a very large proportion of the educated public still receives its impressions of the poet at second hand, from literary hearsay, or the epitomising essays of critics.

To present, therefore, a representative portion of Chaucer's unfinished masterpiece in such form as shall best preserve for a modern reader the substance and style of the original, is the chief aim of this book. When the publishers asked me to carry out this object, the nature of the appropriate form presented itself for solution. As modernisation, the undertaking is not new. At various epochs, and with varying scope of design, poets such as Dryden, Pope, Leigh Hunt, Elizabeth Barrett, Wordsworth, have contrived metrical versions of the Canterbury Tales in the literary forms of their own day. Lesser poets and writers of the past two centuries have executed the like. Their versions possess in common the aim of substituting modern English verse for Chaucer's, often as an alleged latter-day improvement. All, as Professor Lounsbury has shown, "had a direct tendency at the time to divert men from the study of the original." The present rendering, therefore, which is rather a modified form than a modernisation of Chaucer's tales, is believed to differ from all the aforesaid versions in method and, largely, in motive. For the form adopted is prose; it preserves, as closely as possible, the very words of Chaucer and his characteristic constructions; it aims by faithful accuracy to present a text which shall be efficient in promoting the study of the original. In working principle, it has taken advice from the poet himself in his Prologue:

> "For this ye knowen al-so wel as I,
> Who-so shal telle a tale after a man,
> He moot reherce, as ny as ever he can,
> Everich a word, if it be in his charge,
> Al speke he never so rudeliche and large;
> Or elles he moot telle his tale untrewe,
> Or feyne thing, or finde wordes newe."

Briefly, then, the method followed has been to present, so far as possible, Chaucer's *ipsissima verba*; to err rather in the direction of literal fidelity than literary license. No archaisms, however, have been retained which are not fairly intelligible. The necessary changes which have been made are: first, omissions on the score of propriety, of intelligibility (as when a long paraphrase would have been required for a trivial matter), and (very seldom) of redundancy; secondly, rare and slight rearrangements for the sake of clearness; thirdly, translation and paraphrase required by clearness and the necessities of prose-style. Proper names have been altered to their classical or modern forms only in the case of historical characters or places fairly familiar to-day. The text of Professor Skeat has been followed almost always and his notes very largely.

The number of tales selected is the result of the particular scope of this volume, which, as I have said, seeks only to present a representative part of the Canterbury Tales. The choice of the tales has been further limited by the expediency of selecting from among those which are neither too broad (as the Summoner's), nor too prolix (as the Parson's). To the tales chosen have been added those prologues, epilogues, and links which directly pertain to them in the Chaucerian design. The Squire's Tale, though unfinished, has been included for the sake not only of its own romantic charm, but of that familiar citation of its author by which Milton has immortalised its very incompleteness, and taught us of the after-time still to

> "Call up him that left half-told
> The story of Cambuscan bold."

'There remains for me to express—what I should have preferred to signify, in other wise, on the title-page—my grateful acknowledgment of the vital assistance given to this book by Dr. John S. P. Tatlock of the University of Michigan. He has read all the text in manuscript, or proof, and in very few instances have I dissented from his emendations. The insight and supervision of his thorough scholarship have been of the utmost benefit to this undertaking.

PERCY MACKAYE.

The Prologue

Here beginneth the book of the Tales of Canterbury.

WHEN April with his sweet showers hath pierced to the
root the drought of March and bathed every vine in
liquid the virtue of which maketh the flowers to start,
when eke Zephirus with his sweet breath hath quickened the
tender shoots in every heath and holt, and the young sun hath sped
his half course in the Ram, and the little birds make their melodies
and all the night sleep with open eye, so nature pricketh them
in their hearts, then folk long to go on pilgrimages—and palmers
to seek strange shores—to the far shrines of saints known in
sundry lands; and especially from every shire's end of England
they journey to Canterbury to visit the holy blessed Martyr, that
hath helped them when they were sick.

It befell on a day in that season, as I rested at the Tabard in
Southwark, ready to wend on my pilgrimage to Canterbury, with
heart full devout, that at night there was come into that hostel a
company of sundry folk, full nine and twenty, by chance fallen
in fellowship, and all were pilgrims that would ride toward
Canterbury. The chambers and stables were spacious, and fairly
were we entertained; and in brief, when the sun was at rest, I had
so spoken with every one of them that anon I was of their
fellowship, and made agreement to rise early and take our way
whither I told you.

Natheless, while I have time and space, ere I pass farther
in this tale, methinketh it reasonable to tell you all the character

of each of them, as it seemed to me, what folk they were, and of what estate, and eke in what accoutrement; and first, then, I will begin with a knight.

A Knight—a worthy man—there was, that since the time when first he rode out, loved chivalry, truth and honour, courtesy and liberality. Full valiant he was in battle for his lord, and eke had ridden, no man farther, in Christendom and heathenesse; and ever was honoured for his valour. He was at Alexandria when it was won. Full many a time in Prussia he had sat first at board above all the nations. In Lithuania he had warred and in Russia, no Christian of his degree so oft. In Granada eke he had been at the siege of Algezir and ridden into Belmarye. He was at Satalye and Lyeys when they were won; and in the Great Sea he had been with many a noble army. He had been at fifteen mortal battles, and fought for our faith thrice in the lists at Tramissene, and aye slain his foe. This same worthy Knight eke had fought once for the lord of Palatye against another heathen host in Turkey. And evermore he had a sovereign repute. And though he was valorous, he was wise, and as meek of his bearing as a maid. He never yet in all his life spake discourtesy to any manner of man. He was a very perfect gentle knight. But to tell you of his accoutrement, his horses were good, but he was not gaily clad. He wore a tunic of fustian, all rust-stained by his coat of mail; for he was lately come from his travel, and went to make his pilgrimage.

With him was his son, a young Squire, a lusty novice in arms and a lover, with locks curled as they had been laid in press. He was, as I ween, some twenty years of age. In stature he was of moderate height, and wondrous nimble and great of strength. He had sometime been in the wars in Flanders, Artois and

Picardy, and borne him well, for so little time, in hope to stand in his lady's grace. He was embroidered like a mead all full of fresh flowers red and white; all day long he was singing or piping on the flute; he was as fresh as the month of May. His gown was short, with sleeves wide and long. Well could he sit his horse and ride fairly. He could make songs and well endite a thing, joust and dance eke, and draw well and write. So hot he loved that by night he slept no more than the nightingale. He was courteous, lowly and diligent to serve, and carved before his father at table.

A Yeoman had this knight, and no other servants at that time, for he list to ride so. This yeoman was clad in a coat and hood of green, and bore a sheaf of peacock-arrows bright and sharp full thriftily under his belt. He could dress his hunting-tackle like a true yeoman; his arrow-feathers were not draggled out of line. In his hand he bare a mighty bow; and well he knew all the practice of wood-craft. He had a head round like a nut, and a brown visage. On his arm he bare a gay bracer, and by his side a buckler and sword, and on the other side a gay dagger, well harnessed and sharp as a spear-point. On his breast was a medal of Saint Christopher, of bright silver. He bare a horn, with baldric of green. I deem in good sooth he was a forester.

There was eke a nun, a Prioress, that was of her smiling full simple and quiet. Her greatest oath was but by St. Loy. And she was called Madame Eglantine. Full well she sung divine service, full seemly intoned in her nose. And French she spake fair and prettily, after the school of Stratford-atte-Bow, for to her French of Paris was unknown. At meat she was well taught; she let no morsel fall from her lips, nor wet her fingers deep in her sauce. She could carry well a morsel, and take good heed that no drop fell on her breast. Full much she took pleasure in good-breeding. She wiped her upper lip so clean that, when she had drunk her draught, no bit of grease could be seen in her cup; and she reached full seemly after her meat, and in truth she was very diverting and full pleasant and amiable of bearing, and took pains to imitate the manners of court, and be stately of demeanour, and to be held worthy of highest respect. But to speak of her conscience, she was so charitable and pitiful, she would weep if she saw a mouse caught in a trap, if it were dead or bleeding. Small hounds she had, that she fed with roast flesh, or milk and cake-bread; but sore she wept if one of them died, or men smote it sharply with a rod; and all was conscience and tender heart. Full seemly her wimple was fluted; her nose was prettily shaped, her eyes grey as glass, her mouth small and thereto full soft and red. But verily her forehead was fair; I trow it was almost a span high, for certainly she was not undergrown. Her cloak was full graceful, as I was ware. About her arm she wore, of small coral, a set of beads with knobs of green, and thereon hung a brooch of bright gold, on which was writ first a crowned A and afterward *Amor vincit omnia.**

Another nun she had with her, who was her chaplain, and three Priests.

A Monk there was, passing worthy, a bailiff to his house, who loved hunting; a manly man, well fit to be abbot. He had many a dainty horse in stable, and when he rode, men might hear his bridle jingling in a whistling wind as clear and loud as the chapel-bell, where this lord was prior. Because the rule of Saint Maur or of Saint Benedict was old and somewhat strait, this same monk let old things pass, and held his course after the new world. He gave not a plucked hen for that text which saith hunters

10

*Love conquers all.

be not holy, nor that a monk cloisterless is likened to a fish water-
less, that is to say a monk out of his convent; that text he held
not worth an oyster; and I said to him his opinion was good.
Why should he study and make himself mad poring alway upon
a book in a cloister, or drudge and labour with his hands as
Austin biddeth? How shall the world be served? Let Austin
have his drudgery kept for himself. Therefore, in good sooth,
he was a hard spurrer; he had greyhounds, as swift as fowl in
flight; and all his heart was set in spurring and hunting the hare;
for at no cost would he refrain. I saw his sleeves edged at the
wrist with grey fur, and that the finest in the land; and to fasten
his hood at the throat he had a pin curiously wrought of gold,
with a love-knot at the larger end. His head was bald and shone
as a glass, and eke his face as if he had been anointed. He was
in good trim, a full fat lord. His eyes glittered and rolled in his
head, and glowed as the furnace beneath a cauldron. His boots
were supple, his horses in fine case. Certainly he was a fair
prelate; he was not pale as a purgatorial ghost; a fat swan he
loved best of any flesh. His palfrey was as brown as a berry.

A Friar there was, jocund and wanton, a limiter, a self-
important man. In all the four orders there is none that knoweth
so much of dalliance and fair speech. He had made full many
a marriage of young women at his own cost. He was a noble
pillar unto his order, full well beloved and familiar with frank-
lins everywhere in his country, and also with worthy women of
the town. For he had power of confession, as himself said, more
than a parson, for he was licentiate of his order. Full sweetly he
heard confession, and pleasant was his absolution; he was a com-
plaisant man to grant penance, whereso he wist he should get a
good meal. For to give unto a poor order is a sign that a man is

well shriven, for if a man gave, he avowed he wist that he was repentant; for many a man is so hard of heart that he may not weep, although he be sore in pain; therefore instead of prayers and weeping, men may give silver to the poor friars. His tippet was aye stuffed full of knives and pins, to give unto fair dames; and he had in sooth a merry voice; he could sing well and play on the harp. At singing ballads he gained the palm utterly. His neck was as white as the flower-de-luce, and eke he was as strong as a champion. He knew the taverns in every town and the innkeepers and tapsters better than the lepers and beggars. For it accorded not with the dignity of such a worthy man to have acquaintance with sick lepers. It is not seemly, it doth not profit, to deal with such poor rubbish, but rather with rich folk and victuallers. And whereso profit might arise, he was courteous and lowly in serving. Nowhere was there a man so efficacious; he was the best beggar of his order; for though a widow had never a shoe, yet was his *"In principio"* so pleasant, that ere he went he would have a farthing. The proceeds of his begging were better far than his rents. And he could romp like a whelp. On love-days he could effect much; for there he was not like a cloistral monk, or a poor scholar with threadbare cloak, but he was like a doctor or pope. His semicope was of double worsted and fresh from the press stood out round like a bell. For his wantonness somewhat he lisped, to make his English sweet on his tongue; and in his harping, when he had done singing, his eyes twinkled in his head right as the stars in the frosty night. This worthy limiter was called Huberd.

A Merchant with a forked beard there was, in motley, and he sat high on horse, a Flandrish beaver-hat on his head, his boots clasped neat and fair. His opinions he spake full grandly, alway tending to the increase of his own winnings. He would that the sea were guarded at any cost betwixt Middleburgh and Orwell. He knew well how to profit by the exchange on French crowns. This worthy man well employed his wit; no man wist that he was in debt, so stately was he of behaviour in his bargains and borrowings. Truly he was a worthy man, but to say sooth, I wot not how men call him.

There was also a Clerk of Oxford, that had long gone unto lectures on logic. His horse was as lean as a rake, and he himself was not right fat, I warrant, but looked hollow and eke sober. His outer cape was full threadbare, for he had got him as yet no benefice, nor was so worldly as to have secular employment. For he had liefer have at his bed-side twenty books of Aristotle's philosophy, clad in black or red, than rich robes, or a fiddle, or gay psaltery. Albeit he was a philosopher, yet he had but little gold in his chest, but all that he might gain from his friends he spent on books and learning, and busily did pray for the souls of them that gave him wherewith to attend the schools. Of study he took most heed and care. Not one word he spake more than was needful, and that was said short and quick and full of high import, form and reverence. His discourse ever tended to moral virtue, and gladly he would learn and gladly would teach.

There was also a Sergeant-at-law, ware and wise, that had often been at Paul's church-porch. Full rich of excellence he was, discreet and of great importance; or such he seemed, his words were so sage. He was full oft justice in assize by patent and perpetual commission. For his knowledge and his high renown he had many a fee and robe. There was nowhere so great a buyer of land; all proved fee simple to him; his titles

13

might not be made null. Nowhere was so busy a man as he, and yet he seemed busier than he was. He had in set terms all the cases and judgments that had befallen since the time of King William. He could eke compose and make a deed; no wight could pick a flaw in his forms, and he knew every statute in full by heart. He rode simply in a motley coat, girt with a silk girdle with narrow bosses. Of his garb I tell no longer tale.

With him there was a Franklin; white was his beard as the daisy, and ruddy he was of complexion. He loved well of a morning a sop in wine. To live in delight was ever his wont, for he was the own son of Epicurus, who held the opinion that the highest good verily standeth in pleasure. He was a householder, and that a great,—a very Saint Julian in his own country. His bread and ale were alway of one excellence; was nowhere a man with a better store of wine. His house was never without great pasties of fish and flesh, and that so plentiful that in his house it snowed meat and drink and all dainties men could devise. According to the sundry seasons of the year, so he changed his fare. Many a fat partridge had he in mew, and in his pond many a bream and luce. Woe to his cook, if his sauce were not poignant and sharp and all his gear ready. All the long day his solid board stood ready covered in his hall. At sessions he was lord and master, and full oft he was knight of the shire in Parliament. At his girdle hung a dagger and a silken pouch, white as morning's milk. He had been an auditor and a sheriff; nowhere was there such a worthy country gentleman.

An Haberdasher, a Carpenter, a Weaver, a Dyer and a Draper were also with us, clothed all in the like livery of a great and important guild. Full fresh and new their gear was trimmed, their girdles and their pouches. Their knives were not capped with brass, but with silver, wrought full clean and well. Each of them well seemed a fair burgess, to sit on a dais in a guild-hall. Each for wisdom was fit to be head of his fraternity. For they had enough of goods and income, and eke their wives would soon agree; and else they were certainly in fault. It is full fair to be called *"madame,"* and walk to vigils before the rest, and have a mantle borne regally.

A Cook they had with them for the journey, to boil chickens, with the marrow-bones, and with spicy powders and sweet cyperus. Well knew he a draught of London ale. He could roast, seethe, broil, fry, make broths and well bake a pasty. Capon stew he made, no man better. But it was great pity, methought, that on his chin he had a sore.

A Shipman there was that dwelt far in the west; for aught I wot, he was of Dartmouth. He rode upon a nag as well as he knew how, in a gown of serge as far as the knee. On a lace about his neck he had a dagger, hanging down under his arm. The hot summer had made his hue all brown. He was certainly a good fellow; full many a draught of wine he had privily drawn on voyage from Bordeaux, while the merchant slept. For nice conscience he cared not a straw. If he fought and had the upper hand of his enemies, he sent them home to every country by water. But in skill to be wary against danger, to reckon well his tides, his currents, his harbour, his pilotage and his moon, there was none such from Hull to Carthage. He was hardy and prudent in a venture. By many a tempest his beard had been shaken. He knew well all the havens from Gothland to the Cape of Finisterre, and every creek in Spain and Brittany. His barge was called the Maudelayne.

A Doctor of Physic was with us; in all this world there was

none like him for surgery and physic, for he was well grounded in astrology. He watched well times and seasons for his patient by his natural magic; well could he choose a fortunate ascendent for his images. He knew the cause of every ailment, were it of hot humour or cold, moist or dry, and where it was engendered, and of what humour. He was verily a perfect practitioner. The cause known, and the root of his ill, straightway he gave the sick man his remedy. He had his apothecaries full ready to send him his drugs and sirups, for each of them made the other to gain; their friendship was not lately begun. He knew well old Esculapius and eke old Hippocrates, Deiscorides, Rufus, Haly, Galen, Razis, Avicenna, Serapion, Averroes, Damascien, Constantine, Bernard, Gilbertine and Gatesden. In his diet he used measure, with no superfluity therein, but great nourishment and ease of digestion. His meditation was but little on the Bible. He was clad all in sanguine and blue, lined with taffeta and sarcenet; and yet he was but moderate in expenditure; he kept what he won in time of pestilence; for gold in physic is a cordial; wherefore he loved gold especially.

A good Wife there was from near Bath, but she was somewhat deaf and that was pity. She had such skill in making cloth that she surpassed them of Ypres and Ghent. In all the parish was no wife that should walk before her to the offering; but if any did, sooth, she was so wroth that she was clean out of charity. Her kerchiefs were wove full fine; I durst swear they weighed ten pound that were on her head of a Sunday; her hose were of fine scarlet, tied full close, and her shoes full new and supple. Her face was bold, fair and red of hue. All her life she was a worthy woman; she had had five husbands at church-door, to say naught of other company in youth, but thereof needeth not now to speak.

Therewith he brought
us out of Town

Thrice she had been at Jerusalem; she had passed many a far stream. She had been at Rome and Bologna, at Saint James in Galicia, and at Cologne. She knew much of wandering by the way. To speak the sooth, she was gap-toothed. She sat easily upon an ambler, well wimpled, and on her head an hat as broad as a buckler or a target, a foot-mantle about her large hips and on her feet a pair of sharp spurs. Well could she laugh and banter in company. I dare adventure she knew of remedies of love, for she knew the old dance in that art.

A good man of religion there was, a poor Parson of a town, but rich in holy thought and labour. He was also a learned man, a clerk, that would preach truly Christ's gospel, and devoutly instruct his parishioners. Benign he was, wondrous diligent and full patient in adversity; and such he was proved oftentimes. Full hateful it were to him to excommunicate for his tithes, and rather in truth would he give unto his poor parishioners of the offerings at church,—yea, and of his own substance. In scanty goods he could find sufficiency. His parish was wide and the houses far apart, but rain or thunder stayed him not, in sickness or misfortune, to visit the farthest in his parish, great and small, on foot and in his hand a staff. This noble ensample he gave to his sheep, that he wrought first and afterward taught. These words he took from the Gospel, and thereto he added eke this figure, that if gold rust what shall iron do? For if a priest be foul, in whom we confide, no wonder a layman rusteth; and let a priest take heed how shameful is a defiled shepherd and a clean sheep. A priest ought well to show by the good ensample of his cleanness how his sheep should live. He let not his benefice out for gold, nor left his sheep cumbered in the mire, nor ran unto Saint Paul's in London, to seek a chantry for rich men's souls, or to be retained in an abbey, but dwelt at home and kept well his fold, so that the wolf made it not miscarry; he was a shepherd and no hireling. Yet though he was virtuous and holy he was not pitiless to a sinful man, nor haughty and aloof of his speech, but in his teaching wise and benign. To draw folk to heaven by fair living and good ensample was his busy endeavour; unless it were some obdurate person. Him, whatsoever he were, of high or low degree, he would chide sharply for his sin. I trow there was nowhere a better priest. He claimed no pomp and veneration, nor made himself a nice conscience, but taught the lore of Christ and his twelve apostles, and first he followed it himself.

There was with him a Plowman, his brother, that had drawn full many a cart-load of dung. He was a true toiler, and a good, living in peace and perfect charity. He loved God best with his whole heart at all times, in joy or heaviness, and then his neighbour, even as himself. For Christ's sake he would thresh and eke delve and ditch for every poor wight without hire, if it lay in his power. He paid his tithes full fair and well, both of his own labour and of his goods. He rode in a tabard upon a mare.

There were also a Reeve and a Miller, a Summoner and a Pardoner, a Manciple and myself; there were no more.

The Miller was a stout churl, full big of brawn and bones, as was well proved, for wheresoever he went, he would win alway the ram at wrestling. He was short-shouldered and broad, a thick, gnarled fellow. There was no door he would not heave off its hinges, or break with his skull at a running. His beard was red as a sow or fox, and broad eke as though it were a spade. Upon the very tip of his nose he had a wart, and thereon stood a tuft of hairs as red as a sow's ear-bristles. His nostrils were black and wide; his mouth as great as a great furnace. A sword and buckler he bare beside him. He was a prattler and a buffoon, and his prating was most of ribaldries and sin. Well could he steal corn and take his toll thrice of what he ground; yet pardee he had a thumb of gold. A white coat he wore and a blue hood. Well could he blow and sound the bagpipe, and therewith he brought us out of town.

A worthy Manciple there was of an Inn of Court, of whom stewards might take ensample how to be wise in buying victual. For whether he paid, or took on credit, alway he was so wary in his dealing that he was aye before others and in good case. Now is not that a fair grace from God that such a plain man's wit shall surpass the wisdom of an heap of learned clerks? More than thrice ten masters he had that were careful and expert in law, of whom in that house there were a dozen worthy to be stewards of rent and estate to any lord that is in England, and to let him live by his own property in honour, without debt, unless he were mad, or live as sparsely as he list—men able to help a whole shire in any case that might betide, and yet this Manciple hoodwinked them all.

The Reeve was a slender, bilious man. His beard was shaven as nigh as ever he could; his hair by his ears was shorn round, and docked in front like a priest. Full long were his legs and full lean, like a staff; no calf could ye see. Well could he keep a bin and garner, that there was no auditor could prove him in fault. Well wist he in drought or showery season, how much his seed and grain should yield. His lord's sheep, his dairy, his cattle, his swine, his horses, his stores and his poultry were wholly under the governance of this reeve, who by his covenant had given the reckoning thereof since his lord was twenty years of age; no man could find him in arrears. There was no bailiff, nor herdsman, nor any other hind, but he knew his trickery and deceit; they dreaded him as the death. He could buy better than his lord. Full richly had he stored for himself in private; of his subtlety well could he please his lord by giving and lending him of his lord's own wealth, and win thanks therefor—and eke a coat and hood. His dwelling was full fair on an heath; the place was shadowed by green trees. In youth he had learned a good trade; he was an excellent wright, a carpenter. This reeve sat on a full good cob that was dapple-grey and named Scot. He had on a long surcoat of blue, and bare at his side a rusty blade. He was of Northfolk, from nigh a town men call Baldeswelle. His coat was tucked up about him, like a friar's, and he rode ever the last of our troup.

A Summoner was with us there, that had a fire-red, cherub's face, for he was pimpled with salt rheum, and his eyes were slit small. He was as wanton and hot as a sparrow, with scald black brows and scurfy beard. Children were afraid of his face. There was no quicksilver, litharge nor brimstone, borax, nor white-lead, cream of tartar, nor ointment that will corrode and cleanse, that might help him of his white blotches, nor of the knobs on his face. Well he loved garlick, onions and leeks, and to drink strong wine, red as blood. Then he would talk and shout, as if he were mad. And when he had drunk of the wine full deep, then would he speak no word but Latin. He had a few terms, three or four, that he had learned out of some decrees; no wonder— he heard them all day long; and eke ye know well how a jay can cry "Watt!" as well as the pope could. But if a wright should test him in other Latin, then had he spent all his learning, and aye he would shout *"Questio quid juris."** He was a worthy rogue and a kind, a better fellow is not to be met with; for a quart of

20

---

*"The question is, what portion of the law [applies]." A phrase heard often in court.

ale, he would suffer a good fellow to pursue his vices a twelve month, and excuse him fully. Full privily eke could he fleece a dupe. And if he found a good fellow anywhere, he would teach him in such cases to have no awe of the archdeacon's excommunication; unless the man's soul were in his purse, for it was but in his purse he should be punished. "Purse," said he, "is the archdeacon's hell." But I wot in right sooth he lied. Every guilty man ought to dread excommunication, for Holy Church's curse will slay, even as absolution saveth. And also let him beware of a *significavit nobis.* He had at his mercy the indiscreet young folk of the diocese, and knew their secrets and was the adviser of them all. On his head he had set a garland as great as if it were for an ale-house sign; and he had with him a round-loaf for a shield.

There rode with him a gentle Pardoner, of the house of Blessed Mary in Charing, his friend and his gossip, that straight was come from the court of Rome. Full loud he sung "Come hither, love, to me!" This Summoner bare him a stiff bass, that never trumpet was of half so great a sound. This Pardoner had hair as yellow as honey, hanging smooth by ounces like a hank of flax, and therewith he overspread his shoulders, but it lay thin in locks, one by one. In sport, he wore no hood, for it was trussed up in his wallet, and save for his cap, he rode bare-headed, with locks dangling; he thought he went all in the new style. He had such glaring eyes as an hare. He had sewed a vernicle on his cap, and before him on his pommel lay his wallet, brimful of pardons all hot from Rome. He had a voice as small as a goat. He had no beard nor ever should have; his face was as smooth as though it were lately shaven. But in his trade there was not such another pardoner from Berwick unto Ware. For in his wallet he had a pillow-case, which he said was our Lady's veil; he had a scrap, he said, of the sail that Saint Peter had what time he walked upon the sea when Jesu Christ caught him. He had a latten cross all set with feigned jewels, and in a glass he had pig's bones. With these relics, when he found a poor parson dwelling in the country, he got more money in one day than the parson got in two months; and thus by flattery and tricks of dissembling, he made the people and the parson his apes. But, to end with, he was in truth a noble ecclesiast in church; well could he read a tale or a lesson, but best of all, sing an offertory; for he wist well when that song was ended, he must preach and file his tongue to win silver, as well he knew how. Therefore he sung so merry and loud.

Now have I told you in a few words the rank, the equipment and the number of this company, and eke why it was assembled in Southwark at this gentle hostel that is called the Tabard, hard by the Bell. But now it is time to describe unto you how we bare us that same night, when we had dismounted at that hostelry. And afterward I will tell of our journey, and all the remnant of our pilgrimage. But first of your courtesy I pray you that ye ascribe it not to my rudeness in this narrative, though I speak plainly in telling you their words and their cheer; nor though I speak their very words. For this ye know as well as I, whosoever shall tell a tale after a man must rehearse each word as nigh as ever he is able, if it be in his scope, speak he never so rudely and broad, or else he must needs tell his tale untrue, or feign things, or find new words. He may not spare any wight, although it were his brother; he must as well say one word as the next. Christ himself spake full broad in holy writ, and well ye wot it is no coarseness. Plato eke saith—whosoever can interpret him—the word must be cousin to the deed. Also I pray your forgiveness if here in this tale I have not set folk in their just degree as they should be placed; my wit is short, ye may understand.

Our host made great cheer for us one and all, and seated us anon at supper, and served us with victual as well as might be. The wine was strong and well we list to drink. A seemly man was our host, to have been a marshal in a hall; a large man, with dancing eyes; there is no fairer burgess in Cheapside; bold of his speech, wise and well taught; and he lacked right nothing of manhood; and he was eke a merry man. After supper he began to sport; and after we had paid our reckonings, he spake of mirth among other matters, and said thus:

"Now, lordings, in sooth ye be right welcome to me heartily; for by my troth I saw not this year so merry a company at once in this hostel as is here this night. Fain would I make you some mirth, if I wist how. And even now I bethink me of a mirth to please you, and it shall cost naught. Ye go to Canterbury; God speed you; the blessed martyr quit you your guerdon. And I wot well as ye go your way, ye purpose to tell tales and to sport; for truly there is no comfort nor mirth to ride by the way dumb as a stone; and therefore, as I said erst, I will make you some disport and pleasance. And if it liketh you all, with one mind, to stand now by my judgment and to do as I shall tell you, to-morrow when ye ride by the way, now, by my father's soul in heaven, if ye be not merry I will give you my head. Hold up your hands, without more words."

Our counsel was not long to seek; it seemed not worth while to make any bones of it, and we gave him our assent without more deliberation, and bade him, as he list, say his verdict.

"Lordings," quoth he, "now hearken, but I pray you take it

not with contempt; this is the point, to speak short and plain, that each of you on this journey, to shorten our way withal, shall tell two tales, on the road to Canterbury I mean, and on the road homeward he shall tell other two, of adventures that have befallen whilom. And he of you that beareth him best of all, that is to say, that telleth for this occasion tales of best instruction and most pleasance, shall have a supper, at the cost of us all, here in this place, sitting at this post, when we come from Canterbury again. And to make you the merrier, I will myself gladly go with you, at mine own cost, and be your guide. And whosoever shall gainsay my judgment shall pay all that we spend on the road. And if ye vouchsafe that it be so, tell me straightway without more words, and I will early prepare me therefor."

This thing was granted and our oaths sworn with full glad heart, and we prayed him also that he would vouchsafe to do as he had said, and be our governor, and the judge and umpire of our tales, and provide a supper at a certain price; and we would be ruled by his decision in high and low; and thus, with one mind, we accorded to his judgment. And thereupon the wine was fetched. We drank and went everyone to rest without any longer delay. On the morrow, when day began to spring, our host uprose and was chaunticleer to us all, and gathered us together all in a flock, and forth we rode, at a little more than a walk, unto the watering-place of Saint Thomas. There our host began to rein in his horse, and said: "Lordings, hearken if ye list. Ye wot your agreement and I remind you of it. If even-song accord with morning-song, now let see who shall tell the first story. As ever I hope to drink ale or wine, whosoever is rebel to my judgment shall pay for all that is bought by the way. Now draw cuts, ere we ride farther. He that hath the shortest shall begin. Sir Knight, my lord and master, draw thy cut now, for that is my will. Come nearer, my lady Prioress; and ye, sir Clerk, let be your shyness and ponder not; every man, lay hand to!"

Straightway every wight began to draw; and to tell briefly how it was, were it by chance or by fate or by luck, the truth is the lot fell to the Knight, for which everyone was full blithe and glad; and he must tell his tale, as was reasonable in accordance with the promise and agreement which ye have heard; what need of more words? And when this good man saw it was so, as one that was sensible and obedient in keeping his willing promise, he said:

"Sith I shall begin the sport, why, welcome be the cut, in God's name! Let us ride now, and hearken what I shall say."

And with that word we rode forward. And he, with full merry cheer, began anon his tale, and said in this sort.

Here endeth the prologue of this book; and here beginneth the first tale, which is the Knight's Tale.

The Knight's Tale

Jamque domos patrias, Scithice post aspera gentis
*Prelia, laurigero, &c.**

WHILOM, as old stories tell us, there was a duke named Theseus, governor and lord of Athens, and in his time such a conqueror that beneath the sun there was no one greater. Full many a rich country had he won; with his wisdom and his knighthood he conquered all the realm of Femeny, that before was called Scythia; he wedded Ipolita the queen, and brought her home with him in much glory and great splendour, and eke her young sister Emily. Thus with victory and with melody leave I this noble duke riding to Athens, with all his host in arms behind him.

And certes, if it were not too long to hear, I would tell you fully the manner how the realm of Femeny was won by Theseus and his knights; and of the great battle betwixt the Athenians and the Amazons, and how this fair valiant Queen Ipolita was besieged; and of the festival at her marriage and the tempest at her home-coming. But all this I must now forbear to tell. God wot, I have a large field to furrow, and weak are the oxen in my plough. The remnant of the tale is long enough. And besides I would not hinder any of this company; let every comrade tell his story in turn and we shall see now who is to win the supper. So I will begin again where I left.

26

*"And now Theseus, nearing his native land in laurelled chariot after battling with the fierce Scythians..." (Statius, *Thebiad*, xii, 519f.)

THE KNIGHT'S TALE

When this duke that I speak of was come almost to the town in all his pomp and happiness, as he cast his eye on one side he was ware how there was kneeling in the highway a company of ladies, two and two in order, clad in black, making such a cry and such a woe that no creature living in this world heard such another lamentation; and they never stopped their cries till they had caught the reins of his bridle. "What folk be ye that at my home-coming disturb my festival so with cries?" quoth Theseus. "Have ye so great ill-will toward my glory, that ye lament thus and wail? Or who hath insulted or injured you? Tell me if it may be amended, and why ye be thus clothed in black."

The eldest lady of them all spake, after she had swooned with face so deathlike that it was piteous to see and hear: "Lord, to whom Fortune hath granted victory, and to live as a conqueror, your glory and honour grieve us not, but we beg for mercy and succour. Show thy grace upon our distress and woe—of thy nobleness let fall some drop of pity upon us unhappy women. For truly, lord, there is not one of us all but hath been a duchess or a queen; now are we poor wretches, as thou seest, thanks to Fortune and her false wheel that unto no rank assureth well-being. And verily, lord, here in the temple of the Goddess Clemence we have been waiting this whole fortnight against your coming. Now help us, lord, sith it lieth in thy power. I, wretched woman, who thus weep and wail was whilom wife to King Capaneus, who died at Thebes, cursed be that day! And all we who be in this plight and make all this lament lost our husbands at that town while the siege lay about it. Yet now, alack! the old Creon who is lord of Thebes, full of vice and iniquity, hath done scorn to the dead bodies of all our lords, and

27

of his tyranny and malice hath had them drawn on a heap, and by no means will suffer them to be either buried or burned, but in despite maketh hounds to eat them."

And with that word at once they fell all on their faces, piteously crying, "Have some mercy on us wretched women, and let our sorrow sink into thy heart."

This gentle duke leapt from his courser with compassionate mood; it seemed to him his heart would break when he saw them so cast down who were wont to be of such high estate. He caught them all up in his arms, earnestly comforted them, and swore his oath, as he was true knight, that he would go so far as his power might reach to avenge them upon the tyrant Creon, who had well deserved death; so that all the people of Greece should tell how Creon was served by Theseus. And anon he displayed his banner, without more tarrying, and rode forth toward Thebes and all his host behind him; no nearer Athens would he ride, nor take his ease even half a day, but slept that night on the road forth, and anon sent Ipolita the queen and her fair young sister Emily to abide in the town of Athens, and forth he rode; I have no more to tell.

The red figure of Mars, with spear and targe, so shineth in his broad white banner that the light glanceth up and down the field, and beside his banner is borne his pennon of full rich gold, in which was beaten out the Minotaur which he slew in Crete. Thus rideth this duke, thus rideth this conqueror, and the flower of chivalry in his host, till he came to Thebes and dismounted fairly in a field where he thought it best to fight. But to speak shortly of this matter, he fought with Creon the king, and slew him in manly fashion in open battle, and put his folk to flight; then he won the city by assault, and rent down both wall, beam, and rafter; and restored to the ladies the bones of their slain husbands that they might do their obsequies as was then wonted. But it were all too long to describe the great clamour and wailing that the ladies made when the bodies were burned, or the great honour which Theseus did them when they parted from him; to tell shortly is mine intent. When thus the worthy duke had slain Creon and won the city of Thebes, he took his rest for the night in that field and then dealt with all the country as he would.

After the battle, the pillagers were busy searching in the heaps of corpses and stripping them of their harness and garments, and so befell that they found in the pile, gashed through with many a grievous bloody wound, two young knights lying hard by each other, both in one coat-of-arms full richly wrought, not fully alive nor quite dead. By their coat-armour and their equipment, the heralds knew them well among the rest as of the blood royal of Thebes and born of two sisters. Out of the heap the pillagers drew them, and gently carried them to the tent of Theseus, who full soon sent them to Athens, to dwell in prison perpetually; he would have no ransom. And when this worthy duke had done thus, he took his host and anon rode homeward, crowned with laurel as a victor. And there he liveth in honour and joy all his life; what needeth more words? And in a tower in anguish and woe dwell this Palamon and eke Arcite forevermore, no gold may free them.

Thus passed day by day and year after year till it befell once on a May-morrow that Emily, that was fairer to look upon than the lily is upon its green stalk, and fresher than the May with its new flowers—for her bloom was like the rose, I know not which was the fairer of the two—ere it were day, as was her wont, she was arisen and ready clad. For May will have no sluggardry at night, but pricketh every gentle heart and raiseth out of sleep and saith "Arise, and do thine observance to the season." Thus Emily had remembrance to rise and do honour to May. She was clothed all brightly, and her yellow hair was braided behind in a tress a full yard long. In the garden at the sun-rising she walketh up and down, and where she will she gathereth flowers white and scarlet to make a delicate garland for her head, and singeth like an angel in heaven. Close to the garden-wall by which Emily took her pastime rose the great tower, thick and strong, and chief donjon of the castle, where the knights were in prison of whom I told you and shall tell more. Bright was the sun and clear the morning; and Palamon the woeful prisoner was gone up as he was wont, by leave of his gaoler, and roamed in a chamber on high, whence he saw all the noble city and the garden eke, full of green branches, where Emily the fresh and fair was wandering. This sorrowful prisoner went roaming to and fro in the chamber lamenting to himself. "Alas," he said full oft, "alas that he was born!" And so befell by adventure or chance that through a window, thick with many a bar of iron great and square, he cast his eye upon Emily; and therewith, as though he were stung to the heart, he started and cried, "Ah!" At that cry anon Arcite started up, saying, "Cousin mine, what aileth thee, that thou art so pale and deathlike to look upon? What is this cry? What troubleth thee? For God's love, take our imprisonment in patience, for it may be no otherwise. This adversity is given us by Fortune; some evil disposition or aspect of Saturn toward some constellation hath given us this, though we had sworn to the contrary. So stood the heaven when we were born. We must endure it, that is all."

Palamon answered, "Cousin, in sooth thine imagining here is vain. This prison caused not my clamour, but I was hurt right now through mine eye into my heart, and it will be my bane. The fairness of that lady that I see yonder in the garden roaming to and fro is cause of all my woe and crying. I wot not whether she be woman or goddess. Soothly Venus it is, I think." And therewith down he fell on his knees, and said, "Venus, if it be your will thus to transfigure you in this garden before me, sorrowful wretched creature, help that we may scape out of this prison. And if so be my destiny be shapen by eternal word to die in prison, have some pity of our lineage that by tyranny is brought so low."

And with that word Arcite gan espy where this lady was wandering, and with the sight her beauty hurt him so that if Palamon was grievously wounded, Arcite was hurt as much as he or more; and with a sigh he said piteously: "The fresh beauty slayeth me suddenly of her that roameth in yonder place; and, if I get not her mercy and favour, that I may see her at the least, I am dead, I can say no more."

Palamon, when he heard those words, stared fiercely and answered, "Sayest thou this in earnest or sport?"

"Nay, by my faith," quoth Arcite, "in earnest; so God help me, I list full ill to sport."

Palamon gan knit his two brows. "It were to thee no great honour," quoth he, "to be false and traitor to me that am thy cousin and brother, sworn full deep, as thou to me, that never, though we die under torture, either of us should hinder the other in love, or in any other case, dear brother, till death shall part us two; but thou shouldst truly further me in every case, and I shall further thee—this was thine oath and mine also, in faith.

I wot right well thou darest not gainsay it. Thus art thou of a truth in my counsel. Yet now thou wouldst falsely go about to love my lady, whom I love and serve, and ever shall till my heart perish. Now by my faith, false Arcite, thou shalt not so. I loved her first and told thee my grief as to my brother sworn to further me, for which thou art bound as a knight to help me if it lie in thy power; or else thou art false, I dare avow."

Full proudly Arcite spake again: "Thou shalt prove false rather than I. But thou art false, I tell thee openly, for *par amour* I loved her ere thou. What wilt thou say? Thou knowest not yet whether she be woman or goddess! Thine is holy affection and mine is love, as toward a creature; wherefore I told thee my hap as to my cousin and sworn brother. I put the case that thou lovedst her first: knowest thou not the old clerk's saw— 'Who shall lay a law upon a lover?' Love is a greater law, by my head, than may be laid upon any man on earth, and therefore human law and decrees are broken every day over all this world for love. A man must needs love, maugre his head; he may not flee love though it should slay him, be she maid or widow or wife. And eke it is not likely that ever in all thy days thou shalt stand in her grace, and no more shall I. For well thou knowest that thou and I be doomed to prison perpetually, no ransom availeth us. We strive like the hounds for the bone; they fought all day, yet they gained naught, for there came a kite above them in their fury and bore away the bone betwixt them both. And therefore at the king's court each man for himself, there is no other rule. Love if thou wilt, for I love and ever shall, and in sooth, dear brother, this is all: here in this prison must we endure, and each of us take his lot."

Great and long was the strife betwixt the two, if I had

leisure to tell it; but to the point. It happened on a time (to tell you as shortly as I may) a worthy duke that was called Perotheus, and was fellow to Duke Theseus since they were little children, was come to Athens to visit him and take his pleasure, as he was wont. For in this world he so loved no man, and Theseus loved him as tenderly; so well they loved, as old books say, that when one was dead his fellow went and sought him down in hell (but of that story I care not to speak). Duke Perotheus had known Arcite at Thebes many a year and loved him well, and finally at the prayer of Perotheus, without any ransom, Duke Theseus let him out of prison freely to go where he would, on such terms as I shall tell you. If so be that Arcite were ever found by day or night in any realm of Theseus it was accorded that by the sword he should lose his head; there was no remedy. He taketh his leave and homeward he sped him. Let him beware; his neck lieth in pledge.

How great a sorrow he suffereth now! He feeleth the death smite through his heart, he weepeth, waileth, piteously crieth, he looketh privily to slay himself. "Alas the day that I was born!" he said. "Now is my prison worse than before, now am I doomed eternally to abide not in purgatory, but in hell. Alas, that ever I knew Perotheus, for else I had dwelt with Theseus fettered in his prison evermore! Then had I been in bliss and not in this woe; only the sight of her whom I serve, though I might never win her grace, would have well sufficed for me. O dear cousin Palamon," he cried, "thine is the victory in this adventure, full blissfully mayst thou endure in prison. In prison? Nay, but in Paradise. Well hath Fortune turned the die for thee, who hast the sight of her, and I only the longing. For it may well be, since thou hast her presence and art a knight worthy and able, that by some chance of changeful fortune thou mayst attain sometime to thy desire. But I that am exiled and barren of all grace and so out of hope that there is no earth, water, air, nor fire, nor creature made thereof, that may do me help or comfort,—well may I perish in misery and despair. Farewell my gladness and my life!

"Alas, why complain folk so commonly of the providence of God or of fortune, that full oft disposeth them in many a guise better than they can contrive for themselves? One man desireth to have riches, that become cause of his murder or great malady; another would fain be out of his prison, and is slain by his household. Infinite harms follow hence, we know not what we pray for. We fare as he that is drunk as a mouse; a drunken man wot well he hath an home, but wot not which is the right way thither, and to a drunken man the way is slippery. And certes in this world so we fare; much we seek after felicity, but full often we go wrong. Thus may we well say and I above all, who weened that, if I might escape, I should be in joy and perfect weal; yet now am I exiled from my happiness. Sith I may not see you, Emily, I die, there is no help."

On the other side, Palamon, when he wist that Arcite was gone, made such sorrow that the great tower resounded with his clamour. The very fetters on his great shins were wet with salt and bitter tears. "Alack!" quoth he, "Arcite, my cousin, of all our strife, God wot thine is the fruit. Thou walkest now in Thebes at large and heedest my woe but little. With thy prudence and manhood thou mayst assemble all the folk of our kindred, and make so sharp a war on this city that by some chance or treaty thou mayst have her to lady and wife for whom I must needs die. Great may be thy hopes over me that perish here in a cage, with all the woes of prison and eke with the pain of love, that doubleth all my torment." Therewith the fire of jealousy flared up and kindled upon his heart so madly that he turned pale as the box-tree or the ashes dead and cold. "O cruel gods," he cried, "that govern this world with the binding of your everlasting decree, and write on tables of adamant your eternal word, why is mankind more bound in duty to you than the sheep that cowereth in the fold? For man is slain like another beast, and dwelleth in prison and hath sickness and adversity, and ofttimes guiltless. What justice is in the Providence that thus tormenteth the innocent? And yet this increaseth my suffering, that man is bound for God's sake to give up his will, where a beast may perform all his desire. And when a beast is dead his trouble is past, but man after his death must weep, though in this world he have care and woe. Well I wot that in this world is misery; let divines explain it if they may. Alas! I see a serpent, or thief, go at large and turn where he list, that hath done mischief to many a true man. But Saturn holdeth me in prison, and eke Juno jealous and furious, that hath destroyed well nigh all the blood of Thebes, and laid its broad walls all waste; and from the other side Venus slayeth me with jealousy and fear of Arcite."

The summer passeth, and the long nights increase in double wise the pains both of the free lover and the prisoner. I wot not which hath the woefuller calling. I ask you lovers now, who hath the worse, Arcite or Palamon? The one may see his lady day after day, but perpetually is doomed to prison, to die in chains and fetters; the other may go where he will, but from that country he is exiled upon pain of death, and his lady he may see no more. Judge as ye will, ye that can, for now I will stint of Palamon a little and let him dwell silently in his prison, and I will tell forth of Arcite.

Here endeth the first part.
Here followeth the second part.

When Arcite was come to Thebes, full oft a day he swooned; and, shortly to conclude, so much sorrow had never creature that is or shall be while the world may last. His sleep, his meat, his drink is bereft him, that he waxed lean and dry as a stalk; his eyes hollow and grisly to see, his hue yellow and pale as cold ashes, and ever he was solitary and moaning all the night, and if he heard song or instrument of music, then would he weep and might not refrain; so feeble were his spirits and low and so changed that no man knew his speech or voice. And in his acts he fared not only like the lover's malady of Eros, but for all the world like madness engendered of melancholy humour in the cell of fantasy in his brain. And, shortly, all was turned upside-down, both habit and disposition of this woeful lover Dan Arcite.

Why should I endite of his woe all day? When a year or two he had endured this cruel torment, upon a night as he lay in sleep, him seemed how the winged god Mercury stood before him and bade him be merry. His staff of sleep he bore upright in his hand, and wore a hat upon his bright hair, and seemed as when he charmed Argus asleep; and said to him thus: "Thou shalt fare to Athens,—there an end of thy woe is decreed." At that Arcite started up. "Now truly, whatever betide," quoth he, "I will to Athens, nor will I spare for the dread of death to look upon my lady whom I love and serve; in her presence I care not if I die." And with that word he caught up a great mirror and saw his visage all disfigured with his malady, and anon it ran into his mind that, if he bore him low evermore, he might live in Athens unknown, and see his lady nigh day by day. Then he changed his garb and clad him as a poor labourer, and all alone, save for a squire who knew his privity and was disguised poorly as he was, to Athens he went the next day. At the palace-gate he proffered his service to drudge and draw, whatso men would command him. And shortly to speak of this matter, he fell into office with a chamberlain that dwelt with Emily, and was wise and could soon espy who should serve her best. Well could Arcite hew wood and bear water, for he was young and mighty and big of bones, to do what any wight could appoint him. A year or two he was in this service, a page in the chamber of Emily the bright, and Philostrate he said was his name. But half so well beloved a man of his degree was never in court. He was so noble of disposition that throughout the court went his repute; they said it were a kind deed if Theseus would raise his station and put him in worshipful service, where he might employ his virtue. And thus within a while the name is sprung so wide of his fair speech and deeds that Theseus hath taken him near and made him squire of his chamber and given him gold to maintain his degree; and eke from year to year full privily men brought him his revenue out of his country, but seemly and slily he spent it, that no man wondered whence it came. Three years in this wise he led his life, and bare him so in peace and war that Theseus held no man dearer. And in this bliss I leave Arcite now, and I will speak a little of Palamon.

In darkness and in prison horrible and strong he hath lain this seven year, pining in woe and affliction. Who feeleth double sorrow and heaviness but Palamon? Love distraineth him so that he goeth mad out of his wit, and thereto he is a prisoner perpetually, not only for a year. Who could properly rhyme in English his martyrdom? In sooth, not I; therefore I pass on as lightly as I can.

It fell in the seventh year, in May, the third night (as it is said in old books that tell all this story more at large), were it by fortune or destiny (by which when a thing is decreed it must be), that soon after the midnight, with the helping of a friend, Palamon broke his prison, and fast as he might go, fled the city. For he had given his gaoler drink, made of a certain wine with sleepy drugs and fine opium of Thebes, that all the night the gaoler slept, and might not awake though men should shake him. And thus as fast as ever he may he fleeth. The night is short and the day at hand, that needs he must hide, and to a grove hard by he glideth with fearful foot; for this was his device, to hide in the grove all day and by night take his journey toward Thebes, to pray his friends to help him war on Theseus; and, shortly, either he would die or win Emily to wife,—this is the effect and his full intent.

Now will I turn unto Arcite, that little wist how nigh was his dismay till fortune had brought him in the snare.

The busy lark, messenger of morning, saluteth in her song the grey dawn; and fiery Phœbus upriseth, that all the orient laugheth with the light, and with his beams drieth in the groves the silver drops hanging on the leaves. And Arcite, who is in the royal court, chief squire to Theseus, is risen, and looketh on the merry morning; and to do his observance to May, remembering what he longeth for, is ridden from out the court into the field a mile or two, to take his pastime on a courser that boundeth as the flame. And to the grove of which I told you he held his way by chance, to make him a garland, were it of woodbine or of hawthorn-leaves; and loud he sang in the face of the bright sun: "May, with all thy flowers and thy green, welcome be thou, May, the fair and fresh—I hope that I shall find some green." With a lusty heart he leaped from his courser into the grove, and in a path he roamed up and down, where by adventure this Palamon was in a bush, that no man might see him, for sore afeared of his death was he. And he knew not that it was Arcite: God wot he would have trowed it full little. But sooth is said many years agone that "field hath eyes and wood hath ears." It is full fair if a man can bear him steady, for every day he meeteth men unlooked for. Little wist Arcite that his fellow was so nigh, to hearken all his words, for in the bush now he sitteth full still.

When that Arcite hath roamed his fill and sung lustily all the roundel, suddenly he falleth into a study, as do these lovers in their odd turns, now in the tree-tops, now down among the briars; now up, now down, as a bucket in a well. Right as on the Friday, soothly for to say, now it shineth, now it raineth, so can fickle Venus overcast the hearts of her folk; right as her day is fickle, so changeth she her mind. Seldom is the Friday like all the week.

When Arcite had sung he began to sigh, and sat him down. "Alas!" quoth he, "alas, that day that I was born! How long through thy cruelty, Juno, wilt thou war against Thebes city? Alas! the blood royal of Amphion and Cadmus is brought to confusion. Cadmus, that was the first man that built Thebes or began the town and was first crowned king,—of his lineage am I and his offspring by true line, and of the royal stock; and now I am so miserable and so enthralled that I serve poorly, as his squire, him that is my mortal enemy. And Juno doth me yet more ignominy, for I dare not avow mine own name, but I that was wont to be called Arcite now am called Philostrate, not worth a farthing. Alas, thou fell Mars! Alas, Juno! thus hath your ire all fordone our kindred save me only and wretched Palamon, that Theseus martyreth in fetters. And above all this, and utterly to slay me, Love hath stuck his fiery dart so burningly through my heart that my death was shapen for me before my swaddling bands. Ye slay me with your eyes, Emily, ye be the cause of my dying. Of all the remnant I set not the amount of a tare, so that I could do aught to your pleasure." And with that word he fell down a long time in a trance.

This Palamon, that thought he felt a cold sword glide suddenly through his heart, quaked for ire when he had heard Arcite's tale, and no longer would he abide, but with face dead and pale started up out of the thick bushes as he were mad, and said: "Arcite, false wicked traitor, now art thou caught that so lovest my lady for whom I have all this pain, and art of my blood and sworn to my counsel, as I have told thee full oft; and thou hast here cozened Duke Theseus and falsely changed thy name. I will be dead, or else thou. Thou shalt not love my lady Emily, but I will love her only, for I am Palamon and thy mortal foe. And though in this place I have no weapon, but am escaped out of prison only by good chance, either thou shalt die, I doubt not, or thou shalt not love Emily. Choose which thou wilt,—thou shalt not escape."

This Arcite, with full pitiless heart, when he knew him and had heard his tale, as fierce as a lion pulled out his sword, and said: "By God that sitteth on high, wert thou not sick and mad for love and eke hast no weapon here, never shouldst thou pass out of this grove, but die at mine hand. For I defy the bond which thou sayst I made. What, very fool! Think well that love is free, and I will love her, maugre thy strength. But forasmuch as thou art a worthy knight and wouldst contest her by battle, take here my pledge that without knowledge of any other wight to-morrow I will not fail, I swear by my chivalry, to be here and bring thee harness sufficient; and do thou choose the best and leave the worst for me. And meat and drink enough for thee I will bring this night, and clothes for thy bedding. And if so be thou win my lady and slay me in this wood, thou mayst have thy lady, for aught that I can do." Palamon answered, "I consent;" and so, when each had laid his faith in pledge, they parted till the morrow.

O Cupid, out of all charity! O kingdom that will have no sharing! Full soothly is it said that love nor lordship will have no fellow with him. Well Arcite and Palamon have found that. Anon Arcite hath ridden into the town, and ere day-light on the morrow he hath privily prepared two suits of harness, both sufficient and meet for the battle in the field betwixt the twain. And alone as he was born he carrieth all this harness before him on his horse; and in the grove this Arcite and Palamon be met at the time and place appointed. Then gan the colour change in their visages; right as the hunter in the country of Thrace, when the bear or the lion is hunted, standeth at the gap with a spear, and heareth him come rushing in the groves and breaking both leaves and boughs, and thinketh, "Here cometh my mortal enemy,—without fail, either he is lost or I;" so fared they in the changing of their hue, as far off as either could see the other. There was no "good-day," nor salutation; without word or debate each of them helped straightway for to arm each as friendly as it had been his own brother. And after that, with spears sharp and stout they thrust at each other wondrous long. Thou mightest ween that this Palamon in his fighting was a maddened lion; and as a cruel tiger was Arcite; they smote as wild boars, that froth white foam for mad ire; up to the ankle they fought in their blood. And in this wise I leave them fighting, and I will tell you forth of Theseus.

Destiny, the general minister, that executeth over all the world the purveyance that God hath foreordained,—so strong it is that, though the world had sworn the contrary of a thing, yea or nay, yet on a time a thing shall befall that falleth not again within a thousand years. For certainly our appetites here, be it of love or hate, or war or peace, all these are ruled by the oversight above. This I mean now of mighty Theseus, who hath such desire to hunt, and chiefly for the great hart in the spring-time, that in his bed there dawneth on him no day that he is not clad and ready to ride forth with hunt and horn and hounds. For all his joy and appetite is it to be himself the great hart's death; for after Mars he serveth now Diane.

Clear was the day, as I told before, and Theseus, with all joy and bliss, and his Ipolita the fair, and Emily clothed all in green, are ridden royally a-hunting, and to the grove hard by, in which was an hart (as men told him), Duke Theseus hath held the straight path, and to the glade rideth, whither the hart was wont to flee, and over a brook and forth on his way; this duke will have a course or two at him with hounds such as he hath chosen. And when he is come to the glade, in the face of the sun he peereth under his hand and anon is ware of Arcite and Palamon, that fight as it were two boars. The bright swords go to and fro so hideously that the least of their blows, it seemeth, would fell an oak. Who they be he knoweth not, but he smiteth his courser with the spurs, and at a bound is betwixt them, and out with his sword and crieth: "Ho! no more, on pain of losing your heads. By mighty Mars, but he shall die at once that smiteth any stroke more. But tell me what sort of men be ye that be so hardy as here to fight without judge or other officer, as if it were a royal lists."

This Palamon answered instantly: "Sire, what need of further words? We have deserved the death, both of us. Two woeful wretches be we, two caitiffs, wearied of our own lives; and as thou art a just lord and judge, grant us neither mercy nor escape; slay me first, for the sake of holy charity, but eke slay my fellow as well. Or slay him first, for, though thou knowest it but little, this is thy mortal foe, this is Arcite, that is banished from thy land on pain of death, for which he hath deserved to die. This is he that came to thy palace-door and said that his name was Philostrate. Thus many a year hath he tricked thee, and thou hast made him thy chief squire. And this is he that loveth Emily. For I make plainly my confession, sith the day of my death is come, that I am that woeful Palamon that broke thy prison wickedly. I am thy mortal foe; and I love so hot the glorious Emily that I would die in her sight. Therefore I ask my sentence and death, but slay my fellow in the same wise, for we both have deserved to be slain."

The worthy duke answered at once, and said: "This is a short conclusion: your own mouth hath condemned you, and I will witness to it. It needeth not to torment you with the cord, ye shall die, by mighty Mars the red!"

The queen, for very womanhood, gan anon for to weep, and

so did Emily and all the ladies in the troup. Great pity it was, as seemed to them, that ever such a chance should befall for gentles they were, of great estate, and only for love was the strife; and the ladies saw their bloody wounds wide and sore, and they all cried, great and small: "Have mercy, lord, upon us women!" And on their bare knees down they fell to kiss his feet, till at the last his mood was softened; for pity cometh soon in gentle heart. And though at first he quaked for ire, he gan to view the trespass of them and eke the cause thereof, and though that his ire declared their guilt, yet his reason excused them both; as thus,—he thought well that every man, if he may, will help himself in love and eke deliver himself from prison; and his heart had pity because of the women, for they wept ever alike; and anon in his gentle heart he thought and softly said: "Fie upon a lord that will have no mercy, but be a lion in word and deed to them that be repentant and meek, as well as to proud, angry men that will stiffly maintain their trespass! That lord hath little discretion that in such cases knoweth no difference, but weigheth pride and humility alike." And, to make few words, when his ire was thus gone, he gan to look up with smiling eyes and spake these words aloud: "Ah, *benedicite,* the god of love! How great and mighty a lord is he! Against his might availeth no barrier. Well may he be called a god for his miracles, sith he can do with every heart as he will. Lo here! this Palamon and this Arcite were wholly out of my prison and might have lived royally in Thebes, and know that I am their mortal enemy and hold their death within my might; and yet, maugre their two eyne, hath love brought them hither both to die. Look now, is not that an high folly? Who is a fool, but he who is in love? For God's sake that sitteth on high, behold how they bleed! Be

44

they not in a joyous plight? Thus hath their lord paid them their wages and their fees, and yet he that serveth Love seemeth to himself full wise. But this is the best of the story, that she for whose sake they have this merriment thanketh them for it no more than me; by Heaven's King, she wot no more of all this hot ado than doth a cuckoo or an hare. But a man must make trial of all things, hot and cold; in youth or else in age every man will be a fool. I wot it by myself, for in my time, full yore ago, a lover was I. And therefore, sith I know how sore love's pain may afflict a man, and as one who oft hath been caught in his noose, all wholly I forgive you this trespass at request of the queen that kneeleth for you, and of Emily, my sister dear. And ye shall both anon swear unto me that ye shall nevermore harm my country, nor war upon me by day or night, but be my friends in all that ye can. I forgive you this trespass every whit."

And fair and well they swore to him what he requireth and prayed him for favour and that he would be their good lord, and he granted them grace, and thus he said:

"As for riches and royal lineage, out of doubt each of you is worthy to wed when time may be, were she a princess or a queen, but natheless (I speak as to my sister, Emily, for whom you have this strife) ye wot yourselves, though ye fight for evermore, she may not wed two at once; one of you, be he never so loath, must go pipe in an ivy-leaf. She may not have you both, be ye as raging and jealous as ye may. And therefore I assign you terms that each of you shall take the destiny decreed him; and hearken in what wise. My will is this and my flat conclusion, that admitteth no reply,—if it like you, then take it for the best,—that each of you shall go freely where he will, without control or ransom; and this day fifty weeks, no farther nor nearer, each of you shall bring an hundred knights, armed aright for the lists, all ready to contest her by battle. And this I promise you upon my troth and as I am a knight, that whichsoever of you hath the greater power,—this is to say that whether he or thou may, with his hundred that I speak of, slay his adversary or force him out of lists, to him shall I give Emily to wife, to whichsoever of you Fortune granteth so fair a grace. The lists I shall make here on this ground, and so may God have mercy on my soul, as I shall be a true and fair judge. Ye shall make no other terms with me for the joust but that one of you shall be either slain or taken. And if ye deem this well said, tell your mind and be content. This is my end and my conclusion for you."

Who looketh now lightly but Palamon? Who springeth up for joy but Arcite? Who could tell or express it, the joy that is made there when Theseus hath done so fair a grace? Down on knees went every wight and thanked him with all their hearts, and most of all and oft and oft the Thebans. And thus with good hope and hearts blithe they take their leave and homeward ride, to Thebes with its broad old walls.

Part III

I trow men would deem it negligence if I should forget to tell of the lavishness of Theseus, who worketh so heartily to set up the lists in royal manner that such a noble theatre, I dare well say, was not in all this world. A mile it was in circuit, walled of stone and ditched without; the shape was round, as a circle, full

46

of tiers rising by sixty paces, that when a man was set on one tier he hindered not his neighbour from seeing. Eastward there stood a gate of white marble, and westward and opposite right such another. And shortly to conclude, such another building there was not on earth, within so little space. For there was no crafty man in the country that knew geometry or arithmetic, nor portrayer or carver of images, that Theseus gave him not meat and hire to plan and to build the theatre. And for to do his pious rites and sacrifice, eastward above upon the gate he caused an altar to be made and an oratory in worship of Venus, goddess of love, and westward he made right such another in celebration of Mars, that cost many a load of gold; and northward in a turret an oratory rich to look on, of red coral and alabaster white, hath Theseus wrought in noble wise in worship of Diane the chaste.

But I have forgotten to describe as yet the noble carving and the portraitures, the figures and the semblances, that were in these three oratories. First in the temple of Venus wrought full piteously in the wall mayst thou see the broken sleeps and the chilling sighs, the sacred tears, the lamentation and the fiery strokes of desire that love's servants endure in this life; the oaths that confirm their covenants, gladness, hope, desire and foolhardiness, beauty and youth, mirth, riches, spells and violence, lyings, flattery, waste and disquietude and jealousy, that wore a garland of yellow marigolds and had a cuckoo sitting in her hand. All delights, singing, dancing, festivals, instruments of music, fair array, and all the circumstance of love which I have recounted and shall recount were painted in order on the wall, and more than I can make mention of. For soothly all the mount of Citheroun, where Venus hath her principal dwelling, was showed on the wall in portraiture with the lustiness thereof and all the garden. The porter Idleness was not forgotten, nor Narcissus the fair of yore ago, nor yet King Solomon's folly, nor yet the great strength of Hercules, the enchantments of Circe and Medea, nor Turnus, of spirit hardy and fierce, nor the rich Crœsus, caitiff in bondage. Thus may ye see that wisdom nor riches, beauty nor cunning, strength nor hardiness may hold copartnership with Venus, for she can guide the world as she will. Lo! all these folk were so caught in her snare, till for woe they said full oft "Alas!" Here one or two ensamples I let suffice, though I could reckon a thousand.

The naked statue of Venus, glorious for to behold, was floating in the wide sea, and from the middle down was covered all with green waves bright as any glass. A psaltery she had in her right hand, and on her head, full seemly to see, a rose garland, fresh and well smelling. Above her head fluttered her doves, and before her stood Cupid, her son, two wings upon his shoulders, and he was blind, as he is oft portrayed, and bare a bow with bright and keen arrows.

Why should I not eke tell you all the portraiture that was upon the wall within the temple of Mars the red and mighty? All painted was it in length and breadth like to the inner parts of the grisly abode that is called the great temple of Mars in Thrace, in that cold and frosty region where Mars hath his supreme dwelling-place. First on the wall a forest was painted in which dwelt neither man nor beast, with aged barren trees, knotted and gnarled, sharp stumps and hideous to behold, through which there ran a rumbling and a gusty wind, as though the storm should rend every bough. And downward under an hill there stood the temple of Mars armipotent, wrought all of burnished

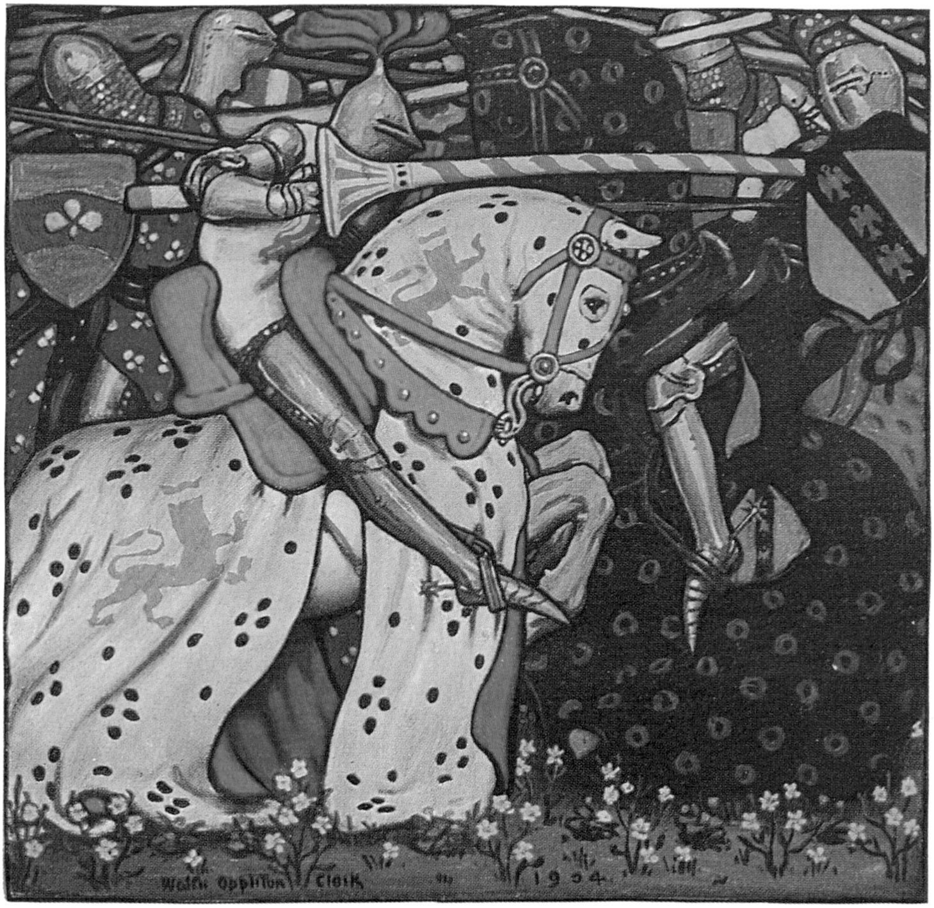

Palamon desireth to slay his foe Arcite

steel, and the entrance was long and strait and ghastly to see, and thereout came a blast and rage that made all the gates to clatter. A light from the north shone in at the doors, for window on the wall there was none. The doors were all of eternal adamant, clamped along and across with toughest iron; and to make the temple strong, every pillar that held it aloft was as great as a tun, of iron bright.—There saw I first the dark imagining of felony and all the consummation; the cruel ire, red as a coal, the pickpurse, and eke pale fear, the smiler with the knife under the mantle, the stables burning in black smoke, the treachery of the murder in the bed, open war with wounds all bleeding, strife with bloody blade and sharp threat. All full of shrieking was that sorry place. The slayer of himself I saw depicted on the wall; his heart's blood hath bathed all his hair. I saw the nail driven through the skull at night; I saw cold death lie with gaping mouth. Amid the temple sat mischance with woe and sorry visage. Madness I saw laughing in his frenzy, armed lament, outcry and fierce outrage; the corpse in the bush with throat cut through; men slain by thousands, the tyrant with his prey reft by force, the town all destroyed. Yet again, I saw burned the speedy ships, the hunter strangled by the wild bears, the sow devouring the child even in the cradle, the cook scalded for all his long spoon. No mischance was forgotten that Mars bringeth to pass; the carter run over by his cart—full low he lay under the wheel. There were also the craftsmen of Mars, the barber, the butcher and the smith, that on his anvil forgeth sharp swords. And all above, painted in a tower, sitting in great pomp saw I Conquest, with the sharp sword above him hanging by a subtle thread of twine. The slaughter of Julius was painted, of Antonius and of great Nero (albeit they were unborn at this time, yet was their death by menacing of Mars painted before in plain image); so was it showed in that portraiture as it is depicted in the stars on high, who shall be slain or else who shall die for love. Let one ensample suffice here from old stories, I may not reckon them all, though I would.

The statue of Mars stood upon a car all armed and looked grim as in a fury, and over his head there shone two figures of stars that be called, in writings, the one Rubeus, the other Puella; thus the god of arms was presented. Before him at his feet stood a wolf with red eyes, and ate of a man. Subtly all this was wrought in reverence of Mars and of his glory.

Now to the temple of Diane the virgin will I haste me as shortly as I can, to tell you all the description thereof. High and low on the walls hunting was depicted and shamefast chastity. There saw I how woeful Callisto, when that she aggrieved Diane, was turned from a woman to a bear, and afterward she was made the lodestar; thus was it painted, I can tell you no further. Her son is a star eke, as men may behold. There saw I Danë turned to a tree—I mean not the goddess Diane, but the daughter of Penneus that was called Daphne. There saw I Actæon turned to an hart for vengeance that he saw Diane all naked; I saw how that his hounds have caught him and devoured him, for that they knew him not. A little further on was painted how the wild boar was hunted by Atalanta, and Meleager and many another, for which Diane wrought him care and woe. There saw I many another story even as wondrous, which I list not draw to mind. This goddess sat full high on an hart, with small hounds all about her feet, and under her feet was the moon, that was waxing and anon would wane. In yellow-green her statue was clothed with bow in hand and arrows in a quiver. Her eyes she cast down full low to that dark region where Pluto dwelleth. Before her was a woman in travail, and full piteously, because her child was so long unborn, gan she call upon Lucina and said "Help, for thou mayst best of all." Well could he paint to the life that wrought it, and many a florin he paid for the hues.

Now were the lists made, and when they were done, wondrous well was Theseus pleased, that at his great cost thus furnished the temples and the theatre. But I will stint a little of Theseus, and speak of Arcite and Palamon.

The day of their returning approacheth, when each shall bring an hundred knights to decide the cause by battle, as I told you. And to Athens, for to hold their covenant, hath each of them brought an hundred knights well and fitly armed for the war. And in sooth many a man trowed that never since the world was made, as far as God hath formed earth or sea, to speak of the knightly feats of their hands, was there so noble a company of so few. For every wight that loved chivalry and would have a surpassing name hath prayed that he might be in that combat, and happy was he that was chosen thereto. For if to-morrow there befell such a case, ye know well that every lusty knight that loveth hotly and hath his strength, be it in England or some other land, would wish to be there. To fight for a lady, *benedicite!* it were a lusty sight to behold.

And right so fared they with Palamon, with him went many a knight. One man would be armed in an habergeon, in a breast-plate and a light jupon. One would have a great suit of plate armour, and one a Prussian shield or targe, and another would be well armed on his legs and have an ax, and another a mace of steel. There is no new fashion, that it is not old. They were armed, as I

have said, each after his own liking. There, coming with Palamon, mayst thou see Ligurge himself, the great King of Thrace.
Manly was his countenance and black was his beard; the circles
of his eyes glowed betwixt yellow and red, with rough hairs on
his heavy brow, and like a grifon he looked about; his limbs great,
his shoulders broad, his brawn hard and arms round and long.
And he stood, as the usage was in his country, full high upon a
car of gold with four white bulls in the trace. Over his harness
instead of a coat-of-arms, with claws yellow and bright as gold, he
had a bear's skin, coal-black and very ancient. His long hair was
combed behind; as any raven's feather it shone black; a wreath
of gold great as an arm was upon his head, huge of weight,
set full of bright stones, of diamonds and rubies fine. About
his car went white mastiffs as great as any steer, twenty and
more, to hunt at the lion or the hart, and followed him with
muzzle fast bound and collars of gold with rings filed therein.
An hundred lords, armed full well, he had in his troop, with
hearts stout and stern.

With Arcite, as men read in stories, came the great Emetreus,
the King of Ind, riding like the god of arms Mars, upon a bay
steed, trapped in steel, covered with diapered cloth of gold. His
saddle was of burnished gold new beaten out. The vesture,
whereon were blazed his arms, was of cloth of Tartary, laid
with pearls white and round and great; a mantlet hung upon his
shoulder, full of rubies sparkling as fire. His crisp hair ran in
yellow rings and glittered as the sun. Bright citron in hue were
his eyes and high his nose, his lips were round and his colour
sanguine, a few freckles sprinkled on his face, betwixt yellow
and black. And as a lion he cast his look. I account his age
at five and twenty; his beard was well begun to spring, and

his voice as a thunderous trump. Upon his head he wore a fresh and lusty garland of green laurel, and bare upon his hand a tame eagle, for his pleasure, white as any lily. An hundred lords he had there with him, all armed save their heads in all their gear, and full richly. For trust well that in this noble company were gathered both dukes and earls and kings, for love and exalting of chivalry. About this king upon each side there ran full many a tame lion and leopard.

And in this wise these lords one and all were come, upon the Sunday about prime, and dismounted in the town. When this Theseus, this duke, this worthy knight, had brought them into his city and lodged them each after his degree, he feasted them and strove so to entertain and honour them that men ween yet that no man's cunning in the world could amend it. The service at the feast, the precious gifts to great and small, the minstrelsy, the rich array of Theseus' palace; what ladies be fairest or best can dance, or which can best dance and sing, or who speaketh of love most feelingly, or who sitteth first or last upon the dais, what hawks perch above, what hounds lie beneath on the floor: of all this now I make no mention. The pith, methinketh, is best to tell; now cometh the point. Hearken if ye list.

The Sunday night, when Palamon heard the lark sing, ere day began to break (though it were not day by two hours, yet sang the lark and Palamon also), with holy thoughts and an high heart he rose, to wend on his pilgrimage unto the blessed, benign Citherea, I mean Venus the honourable and worthy. And in her hour he walked forth softly unto the lists, where her temple was, and down he knelt and with humble cheer and sore heart he said as I shall tell you.

"Fairest of fair, O lady mine, spouse of Vulcanus and

daughter of Jove, thou that gladdenest the mount of Citheroun, have pity of my bitter tears and take my humble prayer in thine heart, for that love thou hadst to Adon. Alas! I have no language to speak the torments of my hell. Mine heart may not express the harms I suffer, I am so confounded that I can say naught. But mercy, lady bright, that well knowest my thought and what harms I feel, consider all this and have ruth upon my pain, as surely as I shall be thy true servant for evermore, as lieth in my might, and hold war alway with chastity. This vow I make so ye help me. I care not to boast of arms, nor ask to triumph on the morrow, or have renown in this joust, or vain glory for mine arms trumpeted up and down, but I would have full possession of Emily and die in serving thee. Find then the manner how; I reck not whether it may be better to have victory of them, or they of me, so I have my lady in mine arms. For though so be Mars is god of battles, your virtue is so great in heaven that, if ye list, I shall fully have my love. Thy temple evermore will I honour, and on thine altar, whatsoever my condition, will I do sacrifice and maintain fires. And if ye will not so, then Pray I thee, my lady sweet, that to-morrow with his lance Arcite may bear me through the heart. Then reck I not, when I am no more, though Arcite win her to his wife. This is the effect and end of my petition,—give me my love, thou dear and blessed lady."

When his orison was made, he did his sacrifice full piously, and that anon, with all circumstance, though I tell not now his rites. But at the last the statue of Venus shook and made a sign, whereby he understood that his prayer was accepted. For though the sign showed a delay, yet wist he well that his boon was granted him, and with glad heart he went home anon.

The third hour after Palamon set forth to Venus' temple, up rose the sun, and up rose Emily, and gan hasten to the temple of Diane. Her maidens that she led thither had the fire full ready with them, the incense, the vestures and all the residue that belongeth to the sacrifice, the horns full of mead, as was the usage; there lacked naught for doing her ceremony. While they censed the temple, full of fair hangings, this Emily with gentle heart washed her body in water from a spring, but I dare not tell how she did her rite, unless it be a few words in general. (And yet it were merry to hear the whole; in him that meaneth well it were no offence, and it is good that a man be frank of his tongue.) Her bright hair was combed, all untressed. A crown of green leaves of cerrial oak full fair and meet was set upon her head. Two fires she gan kindle on the altar, and did her ritual as men may read in Stace of Thebes and these old books. And when the fire was kindled, with pious cheer she spake unto Diane as I shall say.

"O chaste goddess of the forest green, who beholdest both heaven and earth and sea, queen of the realm of Pluto dark and profound, goddess of maidens that hast known my heart full many a year, and knowest what I wish, keep me from thine ire and vengeance, that Actæon cruelly suffered. Chaste goddess, well knowest thou that I would be a maiden all my days, and never be a sweetheart or wife. Thou knowest I am yet of thy company, a maid, and love hunting and to walk in the savage woods, and not to be a wife and be with child. Nothing would I know of the company of man. Now help me, lady, sith ye may, for the honour of those three forms of thy godhead; and Palamon and eke Arcite that love me so sore—this grace alone I pray thee, to send love and peace betwixt them, and so turn away their hearts from me that all their hot love and their endless torment and their fire be quenched or turned toward another place. And if so be thou wilt show me no favour, or if my destiny be decreed that I must needs have one of them, send me him that most desireth me. Goddess of clean virginity, behold the bitter tears that drop upon my cheeks. Sith thou art maid and keeper of all thine own, guard thou well my maidenhood, and while I live I will serve thee as a maid."

The fires burned clear upon the altar while Emily was praying thus, but suddenly she saw a wonderful sight. For right anon one of the fires went out, and took life again, and anon after that the other fire went out black and cold; and as it was quenched it made a whistling, as do these wet brands in the fire, and at the ends of the brands ran out as it were many a bloody drop; for which so sore she was aghast that she was well nigh mad and gan cry, for she wist not what it betokened, but only for the fear hath she cried thus and wept, that it was pity to see her. And upon that Diane appeared, with bow in hand, even as an huntress, and said: "Daughter, stint thy dreariness. Among the high gods it is decreed, and written and confirmed by eternal word that thou shalt be wedded unto one of them that have for thee so much pain; but to which of them I may not say. Farewell, I may tarry no longer. The fires that burn on mine altar, ere thou go hence, shall declare to thee thy lot in this love." And with that word the arrows in the quiver of the goddess clattered and rang aloud, and forth she went and vanished; for which this Emily was all astonied and said: "Alas! what meaneth this? I put me in thy protection, Diane, and in thy governance." And home she went anon as shortly as she might. This is all, there is no more to say.

THE KNIGHT'S TALE

At the next hour of Mars hereafter, Arcite walked unto the temple of Mars the fierce, to do his sacrifice with all the rites of his pagan manner. With high devotion and heart devout he said his orison to the god right thus: "O strong god, that in the cold realms of Thrace art honoured and held for lord, and in every country and every realm hast in thine hand all the bridle of arms and disposest their fortunes as thou wilt, accept of me my devout sacrifice. If so be my youth may have merit and my might be worthy to serve thy godhead, that I may be one of thine, I pray thee to have pity of my grief; remembering that pain and that hot fire in which thou whilom burnedst for the beauty of Venus the fair and fresh and young; although once it mishapped thee on a time, when Vulcanus had caught thee in his net, alas! For that sorrow which was in thine heart, have ruth upon my pains as well. I am young, thou knowest, and uncunning, and with love most tormented, as I trow, of any creature living; for she that maketh me to endure all this woe recketh never whether I sink or float. And well I wot that I must win her by strength upon the field, ere she will show me favour, and well I wot without help or grace of thee my strength may not avail. Then help me, lord, in my battle for that fire in which thou whilom burnedst as now it burneth me, and grant me victory on the morrow. Mine be the travail and thine be the glory. Thy sovereign temple will I most honour of all places, and alway toil most in thy pleasure and thy strong arts, and in thy temple I will hang my banner and all the arms of my company, and I will maintain eternal fire before thee evermore, until the day I die. And eke I bind me to this vow, my beard and my hair I will give thee, that hang down long and never yet felt offence of razor or of shears, and I will be thy true servant while I live. Now, lord, have ruth upon my sorrows and give me victory. I ask thee no more."

The prayer of Arcite ended, the temple-doors and eke the rings that hung upon them clattered full loud, for which Arcite was somewhat aghast. The fires flared up upon the altar and gan illumine all the temple, and the ground gave up a smell most sweet. And Arcite anon lifted his hand and cast more incense upon the fire, with other rites. And at the last the statue of Mars began to ring his hauberk; and with that sound he heard a murmuring full low and dim that said "Victory," for which he gave honour and laud to Mars. And thus with joy and hope Arcite went anon unto his lodging, as fain as a fowl is of the bright sun.

And right anon such strife began in the heaven above, for the granting of these prayers, betwixt Venus and Mars, goddess of love and the stern god armipotent, that Jupiter was busy to stint it; till pale cold Saturnus, that knew so many ancient adventures, found an art in his old experience that full soon pleased either side. Sooth is said, age hath great advantage, in age is both wisdom and experience; men may outrun the old but not outwit. To stint contention and fear, albeit that it is against his nature, Saturn gan find a remedy for all this strife. "Dear my daughter Venus," quoth Saturn, "my course, that hath so wide an orbit, hath more power than any creature wot. Mine is the drowning in the wan sea, mine is the imprisoning in the dark cell, mine the strangling and hanging by the throat, the murmur, the groaning, the rebellion of the churls, the privy empoisoning. While I dwell in the sign of the Lion, I do vengeance and full chastisement. Mine is the overthrow of the high castle, the falling of the towers and walls on the sapper and the carpenter. I slew Samson when he shook the column, and mine be the cold maladies, the dark treasons and the ancient stratagems; mine influence is the father of pestilence. Now weep no more, I shall bring it to pass that Palamon, thine own knight, shall have his lady as thou hast promised. Though Mars shall help his knight, yet ere long there shall be peace betwixt you, albeit ye be not of one like influence, which ever causeth strife. Weep thou no more. I am thy grandsire, all ready to do thy will. I will effect thy pleasure."

Now I will stint to speak of the gods above, of Mars and of Venus, and I will tell you as plainly as I can the chief matter, for which I tell the tale.

Here ended the third part.
Here followeth the fourth part.

Great is the festival in Athens, and eke the lusty season of May kindleth such jollity that every wight jousteth and danceth all the Monday, and spendeth it in Venus' high service. But because they shall be early up to see the great fight, they go at length unto their rest. And on the morrow when day springeth, in hostelries all about is noise and clattering of horses and of arms, and many a rout of lords on steeds and palfreys rideth to the palace. There mayst thou see harness rare and rich, well wrought with steel, goldsmithry and broidering; bright shields, head-pieces, trappings, helms of beaten gold, hauberks, coat-armours; lords in rich tunics on their coursers, retinues of knights; and eke squires nailing heads on spears and buckling helms, putting straps on shields and lacing with thongs, no whit slothful where there is need; foamy steeds gnawing on the golden bridle, and hard by, the armourers running to and fro with file and hammer; yeomen on foot, and many commons with short staves, thick as they may go; pipes, drums, clarions, trumps, that blow bloody sounds in battle; the palace up and down full of people holding talk, here three, there ten, surmising of these two Theban knights. Some say this, some say it shall be thus, some hold with him of the black beard, some with the bald one, some with him of the thick hair; some say this man looketh grim and he will fight; that one hath a battle-ax twenty pound of weight. Thus was the hall full of surmises long after the sun gan spring.

The great Theseus, that was waked from his sleep by the minstrelsy and noise, held yet his chamber till the Theban knights, both alike honoured, were fetched into the palace. Duke Theseus was set at a window, arrayed as he were a god on throne. Full quickly the people pressed thitherward to see him and do high reverence, and eke to hearken his behest and decree. An herald on a scaffold cried "Ho!" till all the noise of the people was done, and when he saw them quiet he showed the pleasure of the mighty duke.

"The lord hath considered in his high wisdom that it were destruction to gentle blood to fight in this emprise in the manner of mortal battle; wherefore to ordain that they shall not die, he will change his first purpose. Let no man therefore, on pain of death, send or bring into the lists any manner of shot or pole-ax or short knife, nor short sword with sharp point for to stab; let no man draw it or bear it by him. And no man shall ride against his fellow but one course with sharp-ground spear, but on foot he may thrust, if he will, to defend himself. And he that is put to the worse shall be seized, and not slain but brought unto the stake that shall be ordained on either side;

thither he shall be led by force and there remain. And if so befall that the chieftain be taken on either side, or else slay his adversary, the tourneying shall last no longer. God speed you. Go forth and lay on hard; with long sword and with mace fight your fill. Go your way now, this is the lord's decree."

The voice of the people touched the heaven, so loud they cried with joyous voice: "God save so good a lord—he will have no destruction of blood!" Up went the trumpets and melody, and to the lists rode the troop in order through the broad city, that was all hung with no serge but with cloth of gold. Full lordly rode this noble duke, these two Thebans on either hand, and next rode the queen and Emily, and after that another troop of sundry folk after their degree. And thus they passed throughout Athens and betimes came to the lists. It was not yet fully prime of day when Theseus was set down, Ipolita the queen, and Emily, full high and rich, and other ladies in rows around. Unto the seats presseth all the rout. And on the west, through the gates beneath the shrine of Mars, entereth Arcite right anon and eke the hundred of his party with banner red; and in that same moment eastward on the field entereth Palamon beneath the shrine of Venus, with white banner and hardy cheer. To seek up and down in all the world, were nowhere such two companies, so even, without varying. For there was none so wise could say that either had of the other pre-eminence in valour or in estate or age, so evenly were they chosen, I trow. And in two fair ranks they drew up. When their names had been read every one that there might be no guile in their number, then were the gates shut and a herald cried on high: "Do your devoir now, proud young knights!"

The heralds leave their dashing about, now high ring trump

and clarion, there is no more to say but on both sides in go the spears full firmly in rest, and in goeth the sharp spur into the flank. There men see who can ride and who can joust, there shiver shafts upon thick shields, one man feeleth the stab through the breast, up spring the spears twenty foot on high, out go the swords bright as silver and hew and shred the helmets, out bursteth the blood with red stern streams, with mighty maces they break the bones. One thrusteth through the thick of the throng, there stalwart steeds stumble and down go horse and man, one rolleth under foot like a ball, one thrusteth on his feet with his shattered spear-butt, and another with his horse hurtleth him down. One is hurt through the body, and then, maugre his head, is captured and brought unto the stake, as was the agreement, and there he must even remain; another is led thither on the other side. And sometimes, to refresh them, Theseus causeth them to rest, and drink, if they will. Full oft have these two Thebans met together and each wrought his fellow woe; twice hath each unhorsed the other. There is no tigress in the vale of Galgopheye, when her little whelp is stolen, so cruel on the hunt as Arcite, for his jealous heart is upon this Palamon; nor in Belmarye is there so fell a lion that is hunted or mad for hunger, or that desireth so the blood of his prey as Palamon to slay Arcite his foe. The jealous strokes bite in their helms; out runneth the red blood on the sides of both.

Sometime every deed hath end; and ere the sun went to rest, the strong King Emetreus, as this Palamon fought with his enemy, gan seize him and made his sword to bite deep in his flesh, and by the force of twenty was he caught, unyielding, and drawn unto the stake. And in attempt to rescue him the strong King Ligurge was borne down, and for all his might King

Emetreus was borne a sword's length from his saddle, so did Palamon hit him ere he was taken. But all was for naught, he was brought in; his hardy heart might not help him, he must needs abide, by force and eke by his agreement. Who shall sorrow now but woful Palamon, that may go no more to fight? And when Theseus hath seen this, he cried unto the folk that fought, "Ho! no more, for it is done! I will be true, impartial judge. Arcite of Thebes, that by his fortune hath fairly won her, shall have Emily." Anon began the noise of the people for joy of this, so loud and high that it seemed the lists should fall.

What now can fair Venus do? What saith she, what doth the queen of love? She weepeth, for wanting her wish, till her tears fall down into the lists. She saith: "Without all doubt, I am disgraced." "Daughter, hold thy peace," Saturn replied; "Mars hath his will, and his knight hath all he prayed for, and full soon, by mine head, thou shalt be eased."

The loud minstrelsy and trumpets, the heralds, that cried full loud, sounded on high for joy of lord Arcite. But be silent now a space and hearken what a miracle anon befell. The fierce Arcite had doffed his helm for to show his face, and on a courser spurred down the long field, looking upward to Emily. And she cast on him a friendly eye, for women, to speak generally, all follow the favour of fortune; and in his heart she was all his cheer. Out of the ground sprang an infernal fury, sent from Pluto at request of Saturn, for fear of which Arcite's horse gan swerve and leap aside, and as he leapt, foundered; and ere Arcite might take heed he flung him to the ground on his head. There he lay as one slain, his breast all crushed with his saddle-bow, his face all black as a coal or raven, so was the blood run into it. Anon with hearts full sore they bore him from the lists to Theseus' palace. Then was he cut out of his armour, and full fair and soon brought into a bed, for he was yet alive and conscious, and alway crying for Emily.

Duke Theseus with all his troop was come home to Athens with all bliss and great pageantry. Albeit this misadventure had betided, he would not discomfort them all; men said eke that Arcite shall not die, but he shall be healed of his harm. And they were even as fain of another thing, that of them all there was none killed, though they were sore hurt, and above all one, whose breast-bone was pierced by a spear. For other wounds and for broken bones some had salves and some had charms; they drank brews made of herbs and eke sage to preserve their limbs. Wherefore, as well he wist how, this noble duke encouraged and honoured every man and made revel all the long night for the strange lords, even as was seemly. Nor was it held that any had been discomfited, but only as at a joust or tourney, for in sooth there had been no discomfiture; falling is but a chance, it is but an ill fortune to be drawn by force, without yielding, unto the stake, one man alone to be seized by twenty knights and haled forth by arm and foot, and eke his steed driven with clubs by men on foot, yeomen and knaves—it was deemed no reproach to him, no man may call it cowardice. For which anon, to stint all envy and rancour, Duke Theseus caused to publish the fame of either side alike, as of brethren, and gave each man gifts according to his dignity, and full three days held a feast, and a long day's journey accompanied the kings out of his town. Home went every man the straight road, there was nothing more but "Farewell, have good day." Of this battle I say no more, but I will speak of Arcite and of Palamon.

THE KNIGHT'S TALE

The breast of Arcite swelleth, and more and more the hurt increaseth at his heart. Spite of any leechcraft, the clotted blood corrupteth and remaineth in his body, that neither cupping nor cutting of a vein nor drink of herbs may help him. The animal expulsive virtue of his natural strength may not void the venom. The pipes of his lungs begin to swell, and every muscle from his breast down is wasted by venom and corruption. To save him availeth neither vomit upward nor downward laxative; all that region is crushed, nature hath now no dominion. And certainly, where nature will not act, farewell physic! go bear the man to church! This is all, that Arcite may not live. Wherefore he sendeth for Emily and Palamon his cousin, and then saith he thus as ye shall hear.

"The woful spirit in mine heart may not declare to you, my lady, that I love most, one point of all my bitter sorrows, but sith my life may no longer last, I bequeath the service of my spirit to you above every creature. Alas, the woe, alas, the pains that I have suffered for you so long! Alas, the death! Alas, our parting! Alas, mine Emily, mine heart's queen, my wife, mine heart's lady and my slayer! What is this world, what would men? Now with his love, now in his cold grave, alone, without a fellow. Farewell, my sweet foe, mine Emily, and softly take me in your two arms, for the love of God, and hearken to my words. I have had strife and rancour many a long day with my cousin Palamon for love of you and for jealousy. And so truly may Jupiter conduct my soul, to speak properly of a lover with all particulars, that is of his truth, honour, knighthood, wisdom and humility, high kindred and estate, liberality and all these virtues, so may Jupiter have part and lot in my soul as in this world wot I now of no man so worthy to be loved as Palamon that serveth you, and will till he die. And if ye shall ever be a wife, forget not Palamon the gentle."

And with that word his speech gan fail. From his feet up to his breast was come the cold of death that descended upon him, and in his two arms the vital strength is lost and gone. The intellect that dwelt in his sick and sore heart gan fade; his sight grew dusky and his breath failed. But still he cast his eye upon his lady; his last word was "Emily, your love!" His spirit changed house and went whither, sith I never came thence, I cannot tell. Therefore I stint, I am not one of the divines, of souls I find naught in this record, and I list not give their opinions of them, though they write where they dwell. Arcite is cold, and may Mars guide his soul! Now will I speak forth of the others.

Emily shrieked and Palamon wept, and Theseus anon took his sister swooning and bore her from the corpse. What helpeth it to tell all day how she wept both eve and morn? For when their husbands be gone from them, women for the more part sorrow so, or else fall in such sickness that at the last certainly they die. Infinite were the sorrow and the tears for this Theban's death, of old folk and folk of tender age in all the town, for him wept both man and child; in truth there was no such weeping when Hector was brought all freshly slain to Troy. Alas, the pity that there was! scratching of cheeks and rending of hair! "Why wouldst thou die," these women exclaim, "who hadst gold enough, and Emily!" No man might gladden the duke saving Egeus, his old father, that knew this world's transmutation, as he had seen it change back and forth, woe after gladness and joy after woe, and he showed him ensamples thereof. "Right as man never died that had not lived somewhere in earth, so there lived never man in all this world that sometime he died not. We be pilgrims passing to and fro on this woful thoroughfare which is the world. Death is an end of all earthly trouble." And over all this yet he said much more to this effect, full wisely to encourage the people to take comfort.

Duke Theseus considered now with all busy care where the sepulture of good Arcite might best be made and most honourably for his rank. And at the last he determined that where first Arcite and Palamon had the battle between them for their love, in that same green, sweet grove, where Arcite made his complaint and suffered in the hot fire of love, he would build a pyre on which he might accomplish all the funeral office. And he commanded anon to hew and hack the ancient oaks and lay them on rows in logs well arrayed to burn. Anon his officers ran with swift foot and rode at his command. And after this he hath sent after a bier and overspread it all with cloth of gold, the richest that he had. And with the same he clad Arcite; white gloves on his hands, and on his head a crown of green laurel and in his hand a sword bright and sharp. He laid him on the bier with face uncovered, and wept so that it was pity to behold. And that the people all might see him, when it was day he brought him to the hall, that ringeth with the crying. Then came this woful Palamon, his hair all rough with ashes and his beard all ragged, in black clothes sprinkled with his tears; and Emily, that passeth others in weeping, the ruefullest of all. That the service might be the more noble and rich Duke Theseus let three great white steeds be brought out, that were trapped in steel and all glittering and covered with the arms of lord Arcite. Upon these steeds sat folk, of whom one bore the shield and another in his hands the spear; the third bore with him the Turkish bow, the case whereof and eke the harness were of burnished gold. And with sorrowful cheer they rode forth at a foot-pace toward the grove, as I shall tell you. The noblest of the Greeks that were there carried the bier upon their shoulders through the city with slack pace and eyes wet and red, by the chief street, that was spread all with black and hung wondrous high with the same. On the right hand old Egeus went and on the other side the duke, with golden vessels in their hands full of honey, milk, blood and wine; then Palamon, with a full great troop; and after that woful Emily, bearing fire in her hand to do the funeral office, as was that time the usage.

High labour and provision full richly wrought was at the funeral rite and making of the pyre, that with its green top reached the heaven and stretched its arms twenty fathom in breadth (this is to say, the boughs reached out so far). First was laid many a load of straw. But how the pile was builded up, and eke the names how the trees were called (as oak, fir, aspen, birch, alder, holm, poplar, whipple-tree, elm, willow, ash, box, plane, chestnut, linden, laurel, thorn, maple, beech, hazel and yew), how all these were felled shall not be told for me; nor how the gods ran up and down, disinherited from their abode in which they dwelt in rest and peace, Nymphs, Hamadryads and Fauns; nor how all the beasts and birds fled in fear when the wood was felled; nor how the ground was aghast of the light, that was not wont to see the sun; nor how the fire was laid first with straw, and then with dry sticks cloven, and then with green wood and spicery, and then with cloth of gold and gems and garlands hanging with many a flower, the myrrh, the incense and all sweet odours; nor how among all this lay Arcite's body, with what riches about him; nor how Emily, as was the custom, put in the funeral fire; nor how she swooned or what she spake or what was her wish; what jewels men cast into the fire when it gan burn furiously, how one cast his shield and one his spear, and some cast of their raiment, and cups full of wine, milk and blood; how the Greeks with an huge troop rode thrice about all the fire with a great shout and thrice clattering their spears, and how the ladies thrice cried aloud; how Arcite was burnt to cold ashes, how Emily was led homeward, how the lich-wake was held all that night, and how the Greeks held the funeral-games; who wrestled best naked and anoint with oil, and who bare him best and came off victor: all this I care not to say. I will not tell eke how they came home to Athens, when the games were done, but I will come shortly to the point and make an end of my long tale.

After process of certain years by general agreement the mourning of the Greeks was all stinted. At this time, I learn, a parliament was held at Athens upon certain points and cases, among which points they treated of having alliance with certain countries and of having fully the submission of the Thebans. Wherefore anon this lordly Theseus sent after noble Palamon, unknown to him what was the cause; but in his black clothes sorrowfully he came in haste at his commandment. Then sent Theseus for Emily. When they were set down and all the place was hushed, and when, ere any word came from his wise breast, Theseus had abode still for a space, he fixed his eyes and with a grave visage he sighed, and thus said his will.

"When the great first-moving Cause had created the fair chain of love, great was the deed and high his intent, and well wist he what he did. For with that fair chain of love he bound the fire and air, the earth and water, within certain limits that they may not escape. That same Prince and Mover of all things," quoth he, "hath established certain days and durations down in this wretched world for all that is engendered here, beyond which days they may not pass, though indeed they may shorten them. There needeth allege none authority, save that I would declare my belief that it is so, for it is proved by experience. Then may men well see by this order of things that this great Mover is stable and eternal; unless it be a fool, a man may well know that every part is derived from its whole. For nature hath not taken her origin from any corner or part of a thing but from a thing that is stable and perfect, and descendeth so therefrom till she became corruptible. And therefore, of his wise providence, God hath so well set his decree that all kinds and series of things shall endure only by succession and verily shall not be eternal. This ye may understand and see by the eye. So the oak, that hath so long a youth from the time when it first beginneth to spring, and hath so long a life, yet at the last it wasteth. Consider eke how the hard stone under our feet, on which we tread, yet wasteth as it lieth by the wayside. Sometime the broad river waxeth dry. Great towns we see wane and pass away. Then ye may see that all things come to an end.

"Of man and woman we see well also that, young or old, they must die, the king as shall a page; one in his bed, one in the deep sea, one in the broad field, as ye may behold. Naught helpeth, all goeth that same road. Thus I may say that all must die. Who doth this but Jupiter, who is prince and cause of all things and turneth all things back unto their proper source from which they were derived? And against this it availeth no living creature to contend. Then is it wisdom, methinketh, to make virtue of necessity and take well what we may not eschew, and especially that which is decreed us all. And whoso murmureth at all, he doth folly and is rebel against him that guideth all things. And certainly a man hath most glory to die in the flower of his excellence, when he is secure of his fair repute and hath done his friend or himself no shame. His friend ought to be gladder when he yieldeth up his breath in honour, than when his name is all paled for age because his prowess is all forgotten. Then is it best for a worthy repute that a man should die when he is highest of fame. To be contrary to all this is wilful; why repine we, why have we heaviness, that good Arcite, flower of chivalry, hath done his duty gloriously and is departed out of the foul prison of this flesh? Why murmur his cousin and his wife at the welfare of him that loved them so? Doth he thank them? Nay, never a bit, God wot, for they hurt both his soul and eke themselves, and yet they gain naught thereby.

"What may I conclude from this long discourse but that after woe I counsel that we be merry and thank Jupiter for all his grace? And ere we depart hence, I counsel that we make of two sorrows one perfect joy lasting evermore; and look now, where most sorrow is, there will we first begin to amend it. Sister," quoth he, "this is my full edict, with the counsel here of my parliament, that ye shall of your grace take pity on noble Palamon, your own knight, that serveth you with heart and will, and ever hath done since ye first knew him, and that ye shall take him for husband and lord. Give me your hand, for thus we decree. Let see now your womanly compassion. Pardee, he is a king's brother's son; and though he were a poor squire, since he hath served you so many a day and had so great adversity for you, it should be considered, believe me, your gentle mercy ought to pass bare justice."

Then said he, "O Palamon, I trow there is but small need of sermoning to make you assent to this. Draw nearer, and take your lady by the hand."

Betwixt them anon was made the bond of matrimony by all the council and baronage. And thus with all bliss and song hath Palamon wedded Emily. And God, that hath wrought all this wide world, send him the love that he hath paid for so dear. Now is Palamon in all weal, living in bliss, in health and in richesse, and Emily so tenderly loveth him and he so nobly serveth her that never was there word between them of jealousy or any other annoy. Thus end Palamon and Emily; and God save all this fair fellowship!—Amen.

Here is ended the Knight's Tale.

Palamon desireth to slay
his foe Arcite ⁘ ⁘ ⁘

The Prologue
of the Nun's Priest's Tale

"HO! good sir, no more of this," quoth the Knight. "What ye have told us, in sooth, is enough and to spare, for a little of heavy cheer sufficeth for most folk, I ween. As for me, I say it is a great distress to hear of the sudden fall, alas! of them who were wont to be in great wealth and ease. But the contrary is joy and great delight, as when a man, who hath been in poor estate, climbeth up and waxeth prosperous, and there in prosperity abideth. Such a thing, as it seemeth me, is gladsome; and of such a thing it were goodly to speak."

"Yea!" quoth our host, "by Saint Paul's bell, ye say right sooth; this monk, he clappeth his tongue with a din, and speaketh of how 'fortune covered with a cloud' something—I wot never what; and also ye heard but now of a 'Tragedy,' and pardee, no help is it for to bewail nor lament that which is done; and eke, as ye have said, it is a pain to hear the heaviness. Sir Monk, no more of this, for the love of God; your tale annoyeth all of us. Such talking is not worth a butterfly, for there is no mirth therein, nor disport. Wherefore, Sir Monk—or whatsoever your name be, Dan Piers—I pray you heartily tell us somewhat else, for verily, if it were not for the clinking of the bells that hang on your bridle all about—by the King of heaven that died for us all!—I should have fallen down ere this for sleep into the slough, however miry it were. Then had your tale been all told in vain, for certainly as these clerks say: 'Where a man hath no audience,

74

it helpeth him naught to speak his mind.' But I wot well I shall know a good tale when I hear one. Sir, say somewhat of hunting, I pray you."

"Nay," quoth the monk, "I list not to sport; let another tell a tale now, sith I have told."

Then spake our host with his rude broad speech, and said unto the Nun's Priest: "Come nearer, thou priest; come hither, thou Sir John; tell us such a thing as may glad our hearts. Though thou ride on a jade, be blithe! What though thy horse be both foul and lank, reck not a bean, if he will serve thee. Whatever be, look that thy heart be merry!"

"Yes, sir," quoth he. "Yes, host, by my spurs! In sooth, if I be not merry, may I be chid." And right anon he hath broached his tale, and thus he said unto all of us,—this sweet priest, this goodly man, Sir John.

The Nun's Priest's Tale

*Here beginneth the Nun's Priest's Tale of the Cock and Hen,
Chaunticleer and Pertelote.*

A POOR widow, well on in old age, dwelt once in a small
cottage, that stood in a dale, beside a grove. Since the
day her goodman died, this widow of whom I tell you
my tale, had led her simple life in patience, for her worldly
goods were few and her winnings scant. By husbanding well
that which God sent her she provided for herself and her two
daughters. Three large sows she had, but no more; three kine
and eke a sheep, named Moll. Her bower was full sooty and
eke her hall, in which she ate full many a spare meal. Never a
bit needed she pungent sauce; no dainty morsel passed her lips.
Her diet was in accord with her petticoat. Repletion never made
her to ail; a temperate diet was her only physic, save exercise
and heart's content. The gout hindered her not from dancing;
apoplexy weakened not her head. No wine she drank, neither
red nor white. Her board for the most was laid with white
and black: milk and brown bread, of which she had a plenty,
and broiled bacon, and sometimes an egg or two; for she was as
it were a kind of dairy woman.

A yard she had enclosed on all sides by sticks, and a dry ditch
without. Therein she kept a cock named Chaunticleer, whose
like for crowing was not in all the land. His voice was merrier

76

than the merry organ-pipes that play in the church o' mass-days, and surer his crowing on his perch than a clock, or an abbey horologe. He knew by nature each ascension of the equinoxial in those parts; for when the sun was arisen fifteen degrees, then he crew, that there was no gainsaying it. His comb was redder than fine coral, and battlemented like a castle-tower. His bill was black and shone like jet, like azure were his legs and his toes, his nails whiter than the lily-flower, and his body like burnished gold.

This gentle cock had under his governance, to perform all his will and pleasure, seven hens, who were his sisters and paramours, and in colour, wondrous like to him; of which she with throat of the fairest hue was named fair Demoiselle Pertelote. Courteous she was, debonair and discreet, and so companionable, and bare herself so sweetly, ever since the day that she was seven nights old, that truly she holdeth the heart of Chaunticleer locked up in every limb of her; he loved her so, that it was heaven to him. Ah! but such joy as it was to hear them when the bright sun gan rise, singing in sweet accord, "My lief is faren in londe," for at that time, as I have understood, beasts and birds could sing and speak.

So it befell, one dawn, as Chaunticler among his wives sat on his perch that was in the hall, and his fair Pertelote beside him, that he began to groan in his throat like one that is sore plagued in his dream. And when Pertelote heard him roar thus, she was aghast, and said: "O dear heart! what aileth you to groan in this manner? Ye are a pretty sleeper! Fie! for shame!"

And he answered and said thus: "Madam, I pray you, that ye take it not amiss. God's truth, I dreamed but now I was in such peril that my heart even yet is sore afeard. Now may God," quoth he, "bring my dream to good, and keep my body out of foul prison! I dreamed how that I was roaming up and down in our yard, when I saw a beast that was like a hound, and would have seized upon my body, and would have killed me. His colour was betwixt yellow and red, and his tail was tipped—and so were his ears—with black, unlike the rest of his hide; his snout was pointed and his two eyes glowed. Even yet I almost die for dread of his look. This, it was, caused my groaning doubtless."

"Avoy!" quoth she, "fie on you, chicken-hearted! Alas!" quoth she, "for now, by that God in heaven, have ye lost my heart and all my love. By my faith, I cannot love a coward! For certes, whatsoever any woman may say, we all desire, if may be, to have husbands hardy, wise, generous, and trusty with secrets; yea, and no niggard, nor fool, nor him that's aghast at every knife, nor a boaster, by that God in heaven! How for shame durst ye say unto your love that anything might make you afraid? Have ye no man's heart—and have a beard? Alas! how can ye be aghast at dreams? There is nothing, God wot, but vanity in dreams. Dreams be engendered by repletions, and fumes, and oft of a man's temperament, when humours be too abundant in a wight. Certes, this dream which ye have dreamt cometh from the great superfluity of your red *colera,* which causeth folk in their dreams to be in terror of arrows, of fire with red flames, of great beasts, lest they bite them, of fighting, and of whelps, great and small; right as the humour of melancholy causeth full many a man to cry out in his sleep for fear of black bears, or black bulls, or else lest black devils catch them. I could also speak of other humours, that work sore woe to many a man in his sleep, but I will pass on as lightly as I may. Lo! Cato, so wise a man as he—said he not thus: 'Give no heed to dreams'? Now, sir," quoth she, "when we fly from these rafters, do, for God's love, take some laxative. On peril of my soul, without lying, I counsel you for the best, that ye purge you both of choler and of melancholy, and that ye may not lose time, though there be no apothecary in this town, I shall myself teach you what herbs be for your health and weal; and in our yard I shall find those herbs which have such properties, by nature, as shall purge you well. For God's own love, forget not this, that ye be full choleric. So beware that the sun in its ascension find you not replete with hot humours; for if it do, I dare lay a groat that ye shall have a tertian fever, or an ague, that may be the bane of you. For a day or two, ye shall eat worms as digestives, before ye take your laxatives, lauriol, centaury and fumitary, or else hellibore (which grows there), catapuce, goat-tree berries, or herb-ivy, that is pleasant to take and grows in our yard. Peck them up just as they grow and eat them in. Think of your fore-fathers, husband, and be merry. Dread no dream; I can say no more to you."

"Madame," quoth he, "gramercy for your lore. Natheless, touching Dan Cato, that hath such a renown for wisdom, though he bade us fear no dreams, yet by my troth, one may read in old books of many men—of more authority, I lay my life, than ever Cato was—who say the very contrary of his opinion, and who have found by experience that dreams be significant as well of the joys as of the tribulations which folk endure in this life. It needeth not to make an argument of this; experience itself showeth it in sooth. One of the greatest authors that men read saith thus: that whilom two comrades, with good intent, made a pilgrimage; and it so befell that they came into a town, where there was such a flocking together of people with such scant harbourage, that they found not even so much as one cottage where they might both be lodged. Wherefore, of necessity, they must part company for that night; and each of them goeth to his hostelry and taketh such lodging as befalleth him. One of them was lodged in a stall, far back in a yard, with oxen of the plough. The other man was well enough lodged, as was his chance, or fate, such as governs all of us in common.

"And it so befell that, long ere day, this latter man, as he slept in his bed, dreamt how his fellow gan call upon him, and said: 'Alas! for here to-night I shall be murdered where I lie in an ox's stall. Now help me, dear brother, ere I die. In all haste, come to me!' he said.

"Out of his sleep this man started for fear, but when he was full awake, he turned over, and gave no heed to this; his dream seemed to him was but a vanity. Thus twice he dreamed in his sleep. And at still the third time, his comrade came, as seemed to him, and said: 'I am now slain. Behold my bloody wounds deep and wide. Arise up early in the dawning, and at the west gate of the town thou shalt see a cart full of dung in which my body is privily hidden. Cause that cart boldly to be stopped. It was my gold caused my murder, sooth to say.' And he told him with a pale and piteous face in every point how he was slain.

"And be sure he found his dream full true. For on the morrow, as soon as it was day, he went forth to his fellow's inn, and when he came to the stall, he began to shout for him. Anon the host answered him and said: 'Sir, your comrade is gone. As soon as it was day, he walked out of the town.'

The three Rogues search in the woods for Death~

"This man now gan to suspect somewhat, remembering the dreams he had dreamt, and forth he goeth without longer tarrying to the west gate of the town, and came upon a dung-cart, all loaded as if to dung some land, even in the same wise as ye have heard the dead man describe. And with a stout heart he gan to cry: 'Vengeance and justice for this crime! This night was my comrade murdered, and lieth gaping in this cart. I cry out upon the officers that should keep and rule this city. Harrow! Alas! Here my fellow lieth slain!'

"What more should I add unto this tale? The people haste out of their houses and overturn the cart; and in the midst of the dung they found the dead man, murdered all newly. O blessed God! just and true, lo! how alway thou layest murder bare. Murder will out; that see we daily. Murder is so loathsome and abominable to God, the wise and just, that he will not suffer it to be concealed. Though it may abide for a year, or two or three, yet murder will out. This is my conclusion.

"And straightway the officers of that town have seized the carter and the inn-keeper, and have them so sore tormented and racked, that anon they acknowledged their wickedness, and were hanged by the neck-bone.

"Herein men may see that dreams be worthy of dread. And certes, in the same book (as I hope for joy, I gab not), right in the next chapter after, I read thus: 'Two men who, for a certain cause, would cross the sea into a far country, were constrained by contrary winds to tarry in a certain city, that stood full pleasant on a haven-shore. But on a day, toward even-tide, the wind gan change and blew right as they listed. Merry and glad they went to their rest and cast in their minds to sail full early. But to one of the men befell a great marvel. For one of them, as he lay sleeping, toward day dreamt a wonderful dream. It seemed to him that a man stood by his bed's side, and commanded him to tarry, and said to him thus: 'If thou set forth to-morrow, thou shalt be drowned; my tale is at an end.' He awoke and told his fellow what he had dreamed, and prayed him to delay his voyage, or even for that day to tarry. His comrade, who lay by his bedside, gan to laugh and to scoff at him boisterously.

" 'No dream,' quoth he, 'may so make my heart aghast that it shall hinder me in my business. I set not a straw by thy dreamings. For dreams be but vanities and trash. Daily men dream of owls, or of apes, and therewithal of many a strange marvel—such things as never were, nor ever shall be. But sith I see that thou wilt abide here, and thus wilfully waste thy time in dallying, God wot, I am sorry; good day to thee.' And thus he took his leave and went on his way. But ere he had sailed half his course—I wot not why, nor what misfortune ailed it—the ship's bottom was by chance riven asunder, and ship and men sank under the water within sight of other ships hard by, that had sailed at the same time as they.

"And therefore, fair Pertelote, dear heart, by such old ensamples mayst thou learn that no man should be too reckless of dreams, for I tell thee that many a dream is doubtless to be dreaded full sore.

"Lo! I read in the life of Saint Kenelm, that was the son of Kenulphus, the noble king of Mercenric, how Kenelm dreamed a dream. On a day, a little while ere he was murdered, he saw his murder in a vision. His nurse expounded his dream to him every whit, and bade him guard him well against treason; but he was but seven years old, and therefore gave little heed to any dream, so holy was his heart. By God's truth, I would give my shirt that ye had read his legend as I have.

"Dame Pertelote, I tell you truly, Macrobeus, that wrote the vision of the noble Scipio in Africa, affirmeth dreams, and saith that they be warnings of things that men see afterwards. And furthermore, I pray you look well in the Old Testament, whether Daniel held dreams to be any vanity. Read eke of Joseph, and there shall ye see whether dreams be not sometime (I say not alway) warnings of things that shall befall afterward. Look at Dan Pharaoh, the king of Egypt, his baker and eke his butler, whether they felt no significance in dreams. Whosoever will search the chronicles of sundry kingdoms may read about dreams many a wondrous thing. Lo! Crœsus, that was king of Lydia, dreamt he not that he sat upon a tree, which signified that he should be hanged. Lo! Andromache, the wife of Hector, she dreamed on the very night before, how the life of Hector should be lost, if he went into battle on that day. She warned him, but it might not avail; he went none the less to fight. But he was slain anon by Achilles.

"But that tale is all too long to tell, and eke it is nigh day; I may not dally. In short, I say that I shall have adversity from this vision, and further I say that I set no store by laxatives, for I wot well they be venomous. I defy them; I love them never a whit. Let us stint all this now and speak of mirth. Madame Pertelote, in one thing hath God given me largely of his blessing, for when I look upon the beauty of your face, ye be so scarlet-red about the eyes, that it maketh all my dread for to cease. For as sure as *in principio**'Mulier est hominis confusio'—my lady, this is the meaning of the Latin: 'Woman is man's joy and all his delight.' For at night on our narrow

---

*"in truth, 'Woman is man's ruin.'" [Chaunticleer, perhaps intentionally, mistranslates.]

perch, when I feel your soft side, I am so full of joy and bliss, that I defy both dream and vision."

With that word, he flew down from the rafter, and with a "chuck" gan to call them, for he had found a grain of corn that lay in the yard. Royal he was; afraid no more; he looketh as it were a grim lion. Up and down he roameth upon his toes, for he deigneth not to set his foot to the ground. When he hath come upon a kernel, he chucketh and then to him run all his wives. Thus royal as a prince in his hall I leave this Chaunticleer in his feeding-ground, and hereafter I will tell what befell him.

When the month in which the world began—the month called March in which God created Adam—was completed, and when there had passed also, since March began, two and thirty days, it befell that Chaunticleer, walking in all his pride with his seven wives, cast up his eyes to the bright sun, that had voyaged in the sign of Taurus one and twenty degrees and somewhat farther, and knew by no other lore than nature that it was prime of day, and crew with blissful voice.

"The sun," he said, "is clomb up on heaven one and forty degrees and more in sooth. Madame Pertelote, bliss of my world, hark to these blissful birds how they sing, and see the fresh flowers how they spring. Full is my heart of revelry and delight."

But suddenly a sorrowful chance befell him, for the latter end of joy ever is woe. God wot, in this world, joy is soon passed away; and the fairest-enditing rhetorician might safely write it down in a chronicle for a sovereignly notable thing. Now every wise man let him hearken to me. This story, I vow, is as true as the book of Launcelot de Lake, which women hold in great reverence. Now will I turn again to my matter.

THE NUN'S PRIEST'S TALE

A fox, that had dwelt three years in the grove, full of sly iniquity, and fore-guided by lofty imagination, that same night burst through the hedges into the yard, where Chaunticleer, the splendid, was wont to repair with his wives, and in a bed of herbs he lay still, till it was past undern, biding his time to fall upon Chaunticleer, as all these homicides will do, that lie in wait to murder men.

O, false murderer, lurking in thy lair! O second Iscariot! Second Genilon! False dissimulator! O thou Greek Sinon, that broughtest Troy utterly to sorrow! O Chaunticleer, cursed be that morn that thou flewest from thy perch into that yard! Full well wast thou warned by thy dreams how that day should be perilous to thee. But what God foreknows must needs come to pass—according to the opinion of certain clerks. I take any perfect clerk to witness, that there is great altercation in the schools concerning this matter, yea, great disputation hath there been by an hundred thousand men. But I cannot bolt it to the bran, as can the holy doctor Augustine, or Boethius, or Bradwardine the bishop. Whether God's glorious foreknowing constraineth me of necessity to do a thing (necessity, I construe as absolute necessity), or whether free choice be granted me either to do that same thing or to do it not, in spite of God's fore-knowledge of it ere it was done; or whether his knowing constraineth only by conditional necessity; with such matters I will not have to do. My tale, as ye may hear, is of a cock that took the counsel of his wife—sorrow befall her!—to walk in the yard, upon that morrow when he had dreamed the dream which I described to you.

Full oft be women's counsels cold. Woman's counsel brought us first to woe, and made Adam to depart from Paradise, where he was full merry and well at ease. Yet sith I wot not whom I might offend if I should blame the counsel of women, pass on, for I said it in my sport. Read authors, where they treat of such matters, and ye may learn what they say of women. These be the cock's words; not mine. I can imagine no harm of any woman.

Fair in the sand lieth Pertelote, bathing her merrily—and all her sisters nigh her—in the sunshine; and Chaunticleer, the noble, sang merrier than the mermaid in the sea; for Phisiologus saith in all sooth how they sing well and merrily. And it so befell, as he cast his glance among the herbs upon a butterfly, that he was ware of this fox, that lay full low. No lust had he then to crow but straightway cried "Cok! Cok!" and up he started as one that is afraid in his heart. For by nature a beast desireth to flee from his born foe, if he see it, even though he hath never before cast his eye upon it.

This Chaunticleer, when he espied him, would have fled, but that straightway the fox said: "Gentle sir, alas! where will ye go? Be ye afraid of me? Me, that am your friend? Certes, now, I were worse than a devil, if I would do you harm or discourtesy. I am not come to spy on your privacy, but truly the cause of my approach was only to hearken how ye sing. For truly ye have as merry a voice as hath any angel that is in heaven; and eke ye have more feeling in music than had Boece, or any wight that can sing. My lord, your father (God bless his soul!), and eke your mother, of her courtesy, have been in my house—to my great ease. And certes, full fain would I do you a pleasure, sir. But I will say, sith we speak of singing, may I be blind if I ever heard, save you, a man so sing as did your father in the morn. Certes, it was from the heart—all that he sung; and for to make his voice the stronger, he would take such pains that he must needs shut both eyes, so loud would he cry, and therewithal stand on his tiptoes and stretch forth his neck long and slim. And he was of such discretion eke that there was no man in any land that could pass him in song or wisdom. I have read indeed in the book of Dan Burnel, the Ass, how on a time there was a cock that, because a priest's son banged him on the leg, while he was young and foolish, made him to lose his benefice. But certainly there is no comparison betwixt his subtlety and the discreet wisdom of your father. Now, for Saint Charity! sing, sir. Let see, can ye counterfeit your father?"

This Chaunticleer gan beat his wings, as one that could not discern the fox's treason, so ravished he was by his flattery.

Alas! ye lords; many a false flatterer is in your courts and many a dissimulator that, by my faith, pleaseth you far more than he that saith soothfastness unto you. Read of flattery in Ecclesiasticus, and beware, ye lords, of her treachery.

This Chaunticleer stood up high on his toes, stretching his neck, and held his eyes shut, and gan to crow loud for the nonce; and straightway Dan Russell, the fox, started up, and snatched Chaunticleer by the gorge, and bare him on his back away toward the wood, for as yet there was none that pursued him.

O destiny, that mayst not be shunned! Alas! that Chaunticleer flew from his perch. Alas! that his wife recked not for dreams! And on a Friday befell all this mischance.

O Venus, goddess of pleasure, sith this Chaunticleer was thy servant, and performed his utmost power in thy service, more for delight than to multiply this world, why wouldst thou suffer him to die on thy day? O Gaufred, dear sovereign master that, when thy worthy King Richard was slain with shot, mournedst his death so sore, why have not I thine eloquence and learning to chide Friday, as ye did? (For in sooth on a Friday thy king was slain.) Then would I show you how I could lament for Chaunticleer's need and torment.

Certes, such cry, or lamentation, was never made by ladies, when Ilium was won, and Pyrrhus, with his sword drawn, had seized King Priam by the beard and slain him (as the Æneid telleth us), as made all the hens in the close when they had seen the sight of Chaunticleer. But most of all shrieked dame Pertelote—far louder than Hasdrubal's wife, when her husband had been slain and the Romans had burned Carthage; she was so full of torment and madness, that, of her own will, she leapt into the fire, and burned herself with a steadfast heart.

O woful hens! even so ye cried as cried the wives of the Senators, because their husbands had perished, when Nero burned the city of Rome; without guilt, this Nero hath slain them.

Now will I turn once more to my tale. This simple widow and eke her two daughters heard these hens cry and make woe, and anon they started out of doors and saw how the fox went toward the grove and on his back bare away the cock; and cried: "Out! Harrow! Weylaway! Ha! ha! the fox!" and after him they ran, and eke many other folk with staves.

Ran Colle, our dog, and Gerland and Talbot and Malkin, with a distaff in her hand; ran cow and calf and eke the very hogs, so frightened were they by the dogs' barking and the shouting of the men and women. They ran so that it seemed their hearts would crack; they yelled as do the fiends in hell. The ducks cackled as if men were killing them; the geese flew over the tree-tops for fear; out of the hive came the swarm of bees. So hideous was the noise—ah! *benedicite!* certes, even Jack Straw and his rabble never make shouts half so shrill when they would slay any Fleming, as were made that day after the fox. Trumpets they brought of brass, of box-wood, of horn and of bone, in which they bellowed and blew, and therewithal so shrieked and whooped, that it seemed heaven would come down. Now, good men, I pray you all hearken!

Lo! how fortune suddenly overturneth the hope and eke the pride of her enemy! This cock that lay, in all his fright, upon the fox's back, he spake unto the fox and said: "Sir, if I were as ye, so help me God, but I should say: 'Turn back, all ye proud churls! A very pestilence fall upon you! Now that I am come unto the wood's edge, the cock shall abide here, maugre your heads. In faith, I will eat him and that anon!'" The fox answered: "In faith it shall be done." And as he spake that word, suddenly the cock brake nimbly from his mouth, and straightway flew high upon a tree. And when the fox saw that he was gone, "Alas!" quoth he, "O Chaunticleer! Alas! I have done you wrong inasmuch as I frightened you when I seized and brought you out of the yard. But, sir, I did it with no wicked design. Come down, and I shall tell you what I meant. I shall say you sooth, so help me God!"

"Nay, then," quoth he, "I beshrew both of us, and first I beshrew myself, both bones and blood, if thou beguile me more oft than once. Thou shalt no more by thy flattery make me to sing and close mine eyes; for he that is wilfully blind when he should see, God let him never thrive!"

"Nay," quoth the fox, "but God give him mischance, that is so indiscreet that he babbleth when he should hold his peace."

Lo! such it is to be reckless and negligent and trust to flattery. But ye that hold this tale to be a foolish story as of a fox and a cock and hen, take the moral, good folk. For Saint Paul saith that all which is written, in sooth, is writ for our instruction. Take the fruit and let the chaff be. Now, good God, if it be thy will, as my lord archbishop saith, then make us all good people and bring us to thy heavenly bliss.—Amen.

Here is ended the Nun's Priest's Tale.

Epilogue to the Nun's Priest's Tale

"Sir Nun's Priest," said our host anon, "blessed be thy breech! This was a merry tale of Chaunticleer. But if thou were secular, by my truth, thou wouldst be a lusty fellow with the dames. See what brawn hath this gentle priest, so great a neck and such a broad breast! He glanceth with his eyes like a sparrow-hawk. He needeth not to dye his colour with brasil, nor with dye of Portugal. Now, sir, fair befall you for your tale."

And after that, with a look full merry, he said to another as ye shall hear.

The Physician's Tale

Here followeth the Physician's Tale.

THERE was once, as Titus Livius telleth, a knight called
Virginius, full of honour and worthiness, strong in his
friends and of great wealth. This knight had by his wife
a daughter; no children more had he in all his days. In excellent
beauty, this maid was fair above every wight that men may
see; for Nature with sovereign care hath formed her in so great
excellence as though she would say: "Lo! I, Nature, thus can
I form and paint a breathing being when I list; who can imitate
me? Not Pygmalion, though aye he forge and beat, or grave,
or paint; for I dare well say that Apelles and Zeuxis should
work in vain if they presumed to imitate me by graving or
painting or forging or beating. For he that is the chief Creator
hath made me his vicar-general to form and paint earthly creatures even as I list, and each thing under the moon that waxeth
and waneth is in my care, and for my work I will ask nothing;
my lord and I be fully of one accord. For the worship of my
sovereign I made her; so do I all my other creatures, whatsoever
colour or shape they have." Thus it seemeth me Nature would
say.

This maid was two and twelve years of age, in whom Nature
had such joy. For as she can paint a lily white and a rose red
even with such art she hath painted this noble creature ere she
was born, upon her noble limbs, where by right such colours

should be; and Phœbus hath dyed her thick tresses like to the streams of his lustrous heat. And if her beauty was excellent she was a thousand-fold more virtuous. She lacked no quality that discernment may praise; as well in spirit as in body she was chaste; wherefore she flowered in virginity with all humility and abstinence, with all temperance and patience, and eke sobriety of bearing and garb. In answering she was alway discreet, though she might be as wise as Pallas, I dare say. Her faculty of speech was full womanly and plain; she had no counterfeited terms, to seem wise, but she spake after her station, and all her words, both more and less, were full of virtue and of nobility. Shamefast she was in the shamefastness of a maiden, constant in heart and ever busy to drive out sluggard idleness. Of her mouth Bacchus had no mastery; for wine and youth cause Venus increase, even as men will cast oil into fire. And of her own free will and virtue, she hath full oft feigned her sick because she would flee the company where folly was like to be treated of, as at feasts, dances and revels, that be the occasions of dalliance. Such things, as men may see, make children too soon ripe and bold, which is full perilous and hath ever been. For all too soon she may learn lore of boldness, when she is waxed a wife.

And ye mistresses in your old age that have lords' daughters in governance, take no displeasure of my words. Think that ye be set to govern the daughters of lords only for two things: either for ye have kept your virtue, or else ye have fallen into frailty and know well enough the old dance and have fully forsaken such misconduct forevermore. Therefore, for Christ's sake, look that ye be not slack to teach them virtue. A thief of venison that hath given over his appetite and all his old craft, can keep a forest best of all men. Keep them well now, for if ye will, ye can. Look well that ye give assent unto no vice, lest ye be damned for your wicked mind, for whosoever doth, in sooth, is a traitor. And pay heed to that I shall say: of all treasons the sovereign plague is when a wight betrayeth innocence. Ye fathers and eke ye mothers, that have children, be it one or two, yours is all the charge to watch over them while they be under your governance. Beware, by the ensample of your living or by your neglect of chastisement, that they perish not; for I dare well say that if they do, ye shall rue it dearly. Under a soft and negligent shepherd, the wolf hath torn in pieces many a sheep and lamb. One ensample sufficeth now, for I must turn again to my matter.

This maid, of whom I will tell this tale, so kept herself that she needed no mistress. For in her living, as in a book, maidens might read every good word or act that belongeth to a virtuous maid; she was so prudent and so kind. Wherefore the fame sprang out far on every side both of her beauty and her goodness; that throughout that land everyone praised her that loved virtue, save envy alone that is sorry for the weal of another man, and glad of his sorrow and his misfortune. (The doctor, Saint Augustine, maketh this description of envy.) This maid on a day went to a temple with her dear mother, as is the wont of young maidens.

Now there was a justice then in that town that was governor of that country. And so befell this judge cast his eyes upon this maid, considering her full closely as she came past where he was. Straightway his heart changed and his mood, he was so caught with the beauty of this maiden, and full privily he said to himself, "This maid shall be mine in spite of any man."

Anon the fiend glided suddenly into his heart and taught him that he might by craft win the maiden to his purpose. For certes, it seemed to him, that by no force nor suborning could he speed. For she was strong of friends and eke she was confirmed in such sovereign goodness that he knew well he might never so achieve as to make her sin with her body. Wherefore, upon great deliberation, he sent for a churl in that town whom he knew for a fellow subtle and bold. This judge hath said his say to this churl in secret wise, and made him swear he should tell it to no creature, and if he did he should lose his head. When this cursed plan was assented to, glad was this judge and made him great cheer, and gave him gifts precious and fine. When all this plot was shapen, from point to point, how that his lechery should be performed full subtly, as ye shall afterwards openly hear, home goeth the churl, that was named Claudius. This false judge called Apius (so was he named, for this is no fable, but known for a notable historical thing; the substance of it is sooth, out of doubt), this false judge now goeth about to hasten his delight all that he may. And so it befell soon after, as the book telleth us, that this false judge sat in his consistory, as he was wont, and gave his judgments on sundry cases. This false churl came forth in full great haste and said, "Lord, if it be your will, do me justice upon this rueful petition, in which I make complaint against Virginius, and if he will say that it is not so, I will prove it, and find good witness that what my bill declareth is sooth."

The judge answered, "Of this I may not in his absence give final judgment. Let him be called and I will gladly listen. Thou shalt have right and no wrong here."

Virginius came, that he might know the judge's will, and

straightway this cursed petition was read; the sense of it was as ye shall hear.

"To you, my lord, Sir Apius, sheweth your poor servant Claudius how a knight called Virginius, against the law and all equity, holdeth expressly against my will my servant, by law my thrall, that was stolen from my house by night while she was full young; this will I prove by witness, lord, so it offend you not. She is not his daughter, whatsoever he saith. Wherefore I pray to you, my lord judge, yield me my thrall, if it be your will." Lo! this was the sense of his petition.

Virginius gan look on the churl, but hastily ere he told his tale and would have proved as a knight should, and eke by many a witness, that what his accuser had said was false, this cursed judge would tarry no whit nor hear a word from Virginius, but gave his judgment and said, "I decree that straightway this churl have his servant; thou shalt keep her in thy house no longer. Go bring her forth and put her here in our charge. The churl shall have his thrall; this I award him."

When Virginius, this worthy knight, by the sentence of this justice, must needs give his dear daughter unto the judge to live in lechery, he goeth home and sitteth him in his hall and straightway letteth his dear daughter be summoned, and with a face dead as cold ashes he gan gaze upon her humble face with a father's pity sticking through his heart, albeit he would not swerve from his purpose.

"Daughter," quoth he, "Virginia, there be two ways, either death or shame, that thou must suffer. Alas! that I was born! For never thou deservedst to die with a sword. O dear daughter, ender of my life, whom I have fostered up with such gladness that thou wert never out of my remembrance! O daughter, that art my last woe, and eke in my life my last joy, O gem of chastity, take thou in patience thy death, for this is my judgment. For love and not for hate, thou must die. My wretched hand must smite off thy head. Alas! that ever Apius saw thee. Thus hath he falsely judged thee to-day," and told her all the case as ye have already heard; it needeth not to tell it more.

"O mercy, dear father," quoth this maid, and with that word she laid both her arms about his neck, as she wont to do. The tears burst from her eyes and she said, "Good father, shall I die? Is there no grace? Is there no help?"

"No, certes, my dear daughter," quoth he. "Then give me leisure, father mine, a little while to lament my death, for Jepthah, pardee, gave his daughter grace to lament, ere he slew her, alas! And God wot it was nothing her fault, but because she ran first to greet her father to welcome him with festivity." And with that word straightway she fell swooning, and after her swooning had left her, she riseth up and saith to her father, "Blessed be God, I shall die a maiden. Give me my death ere I have shame. Do your will with your child, for God's sake." And with that she besought him many times that with his sword he would smite softly, and thereupon she fell down in a swoon. With full sorrowful heart and will, her father smote off her head, and took it by the top and gan present it to the judge as he sat yet judging in consistory. And when the judge saw it, as saith the book, he bade men take him and hang him at once. But straightway a thousand people thronged in to save the knight for ruth and compassion, for the false iniquity was known. The people hath straightway suspected, from the manner of the churl's challenge, that this thing was by Apius' consent. They wist well that he was lustful. For which they went unto him and anon cast him in a prison, where he slew himself. And Claudius, his servant, was doomed to hang on a tree; but that Virginius, of his pity, so prayed for him that he was exiled; else certes, he had been destroyed. The remnant, high and low, were hanged, that were privy to this cursedness. Here many men see how sin hath its deserts! Beware, for no man knoweth whom God will smite, nor in what wise the worm of conscience may writhe within a man, though his wicked life be so privy that no man knoweth thereof but God and him. For be he a man simple or learned, he wot not how soon he shall be afeard. Therefore I rede you take this counsel: forsake sin ere sin forsake you.

Here endeth the Physician's Tale.

Words of the Host

The words of the Host to the Physician and the Pardoner.

OUR host gan swear as he were mad. "Harrow! by nails and by blood!" quoth he, "this was a false churl and a false justice! As shameful death as heart may conceive come upon these judges and their advocates. Natheless this poor maid is slain, alas! Too dear she bought her beauty! Wherefore I say that alway, as men may witness, the gifts of fortune or nature be cause of death to many a wight. Verily her beauty was her death. Alas! so pitifully as she was slain! Of both these gifts that I speak of, men have full oft more harm than profit. But truly, my own master dear, this is a piteous tale for to hearken to. But natheless, pass over, it is no matter. I pray to God save thy gentle corse, and thy Galens and eke thine Hippocrates, and every box full of thine electuary. God and our Lady bless them! Thou art a proper man, as I live, and like a prelate, by Saint Ronyan! Said I not well? I cannot speak in clerkly terms, but I wot well thou makest me so to grieve that I almost have caught a spasm about my heart. By Corpus bones! unless I have physic or a draught of musty and corny ale, or else hear anon a merry story, my heart is broken for pity of this maid. Thou *bel amy,* thou Pardoner, tell us straightway some mirth or jests."

"It shall be done!" quoth he, "by Saint Ronyan. But first here at this ale-stake," quoth he, "I will drink and eat of a loaf."

But straightway these gentles gan exclaim, "Nay! let him tell us no ribaldry. Tell us some moral thing that we may learn some wisdom, and then we will gladly hear." "I agree, sure," quoth he, "but I must ponder on some virtuous thing—while I drink."

Here followeth the Prologue of the Pardoner's Tale

Radix malorum est cupiditas.[*]

"LORDINGS," quoth he, "when I preach in churches I take pains to have a stately utterance, and ring it out roundly as a bell, for all that I say I know by heart. My theme is alway the same—'*Radix malorum est cupiditas.*'

"First I announce whence I come, and then I show my bulls, one and all. First I show our liege lord's seal on my patent, to protect my body, that no man, neither priest nor clerk, may be so bold as to disturb me in Christ's holy labours; and then after that I say my say; I show bulls of popes and cardinals, of patriarchs and bishops; and I speak a few words in Latin to colour my preaching and to stir men to devotion. Then I show forth my long crystal boxes crammed full of clouts and bones; they be relics, as each man weeneth. Then I have in latten a shoulder-bone which came from an holy Jew's sheep. 'Good men,' say I, 'pay heed to my words! If this bone be washed in any well, and cow or calf or sheep or ox be swollen of any worm or worm's sting, take water of that well and wash his tongue, and anon he is sound; and eke of pox and of scab and every sore shall every sheep be cured that drinketh a draught of this well; pay heed to what I say. If the goodman that owneth the beasts will every week, fasting, ere the cock croweth, drink a draught of this well as that holy Jew taught our elders, his beasts and his stock shall multiply. And, sirs, jealousy also it healeth.

101

[*]"Love of money is the root of all evil." (1 *Timothy* 6).

For though a man be fallen into a jealous fit, let his pottage be made with this water and never shall he mistrust his wife more, though he knew the sooth of her fault, even had she taken two or three priests. Here ye may see a mitten eke; he that will put his hand in this mitten shall have multiplying of his grain when he hath sown, be it wheat or barley, if so be he offer pence, or else groats. Good men and women, one thing I warn you. If any wight be now in this church that hath done horrible sin, that he dare not for shame be shriven of it, or any woman, be she old or young, that hath hoodwinked her husband, such folk shall have no power nor grace to offer for my relics here. And whosoever findeth himself free from such fault let him come and offer in God's name, and I will assoil him by the authority which was granted me by bull.'

"By this trick I have won an hundred mark year by year, since I was a pardoner. I stand like a clerk in my pulpit, and when the lay people be set down, I preach as ye have heard and tell an hundred more false deceits. Then briskly I stretch forth my neck, and east and west I nod upon the people, like a dove sitting on a barn. My hands and my tongue go so nimbly that it is joy to see my diligence. My preaching is all of avarice and such cursedness, to make them generous to give their pence, and especially to me. For my purpose is naught but gain, and not a whit correction of sin. I reck never, when they be in their graves, though their souls go a-blackberrying! For certes many a preaching cometh full oft of evil intention: one man to please folk and flatter them, to be advanced by hypocrisy, one for vain glory and another for hate. For when I dare quarrel with a man in none other wise, then will I sting him with my bitter tongue in preaching, so that he shall not escape being falsely defamed, if he hath trespassed to me or my brethren. For though I tell not his own name, men shall know well who is the man by signs and other circumstances. Thus I quit folk that do us displeasure. Thus I spit out my venom under colour of holiness, to seem holy and true.

"But I will shortly describe my purpose. I preach of nothing but covetousness. Therefore my theme ever was and yet is, *Radix malorum est cupiditas.* Thus I can preach against that same sin which I practise, and that is avarice. Though of that sin myself be guilty, yet I can make other folk to cast off avarice, and sore to repent; but that is not my principal aim; I preach nothing but for covetousness. That ought to suffice of this matter.

"Then I tell them many an ensample from old stories, of long time ago. For simple people love old tales. Such things they can well report and remember. What? trow ye whiles I preach and win gold and silver by my words, that I will live wilfully in poverty? Nay, nay, truly I thought of it never. For I will preach in sundry regions and beg. I will do no labour with my hands, nor make baskets and live thereby, because I would not idly beg. I will follow none of the apostles; I will have money, wool, wheat and cheese, although the poorest lad give it, or the poorest widow in a village, though her children die for famine. Nay, I will drink liquor of the grape and in every town have a jolly wench. But hark, lordings, in conclusion, your will is that I tell some story. Now that I have drunk a draught of corny ale, by God's light, I hope I shall tell you somewhat that shall by reason be to your liking. For though I myself be a full vicious man, yet I can tell you a moral tale, which I am wont to preach for gain. Hold your peace now. I will begin my tale."

The Pardoner's Tale

WHILOM in Flanders there was a company of young folk, that amidst riot and gambling gave themselves up to folly in the stews and taverns, where to harps, lutes and citterns day and night they danced and played at dice, and therewithal ate and drank to sad excess. In this cursed wise with abominable debauchery did they sacrifice to the devil in his temple, and made use of oaths so huge and damnable that it was grisly to hear them swear. Our Lord's blessed body they dismembered as though they thought the Jews had rended him not enough, and each laughed at the sins of the others. And right anon come girl-tumblers slender and comely, young wenches selling fruit, singers with harps, bawds and wafer-sellers, which be the very devil's officers for kindling and blowing the fire of luxury, which is next door to gluttony. For I take the holy writ to my witness that in wine and drunkenness is lust.

Lo! drunken Lot! Lo! Herod (whosoever will observe the story), when he was replete of wine at his feast, gave command right at his own table that the Baptist John, full guiltless, be slain. Seneca saith eke a good word; he saith he can see no difference betwixt a man that is out of his mind and a man that is drunk, save that madness in a rogue persevereth longer than doth drunkenness. O cursed gluttony! O first cause of our fall! O origin of our damnation, till Christ redeemed us with his blood. Lo! to speak short, how dearly bought was that cursed sin. For the sake of gluttony all this world was corrupt. Adam our father and eke his wife, there is no doubt, were for that sin

104

driven from Paradise to labour and to woe; for while Adam fasted, as I have read, he was in Paradise; and when he ate the forbidden fruit of the tree, he was straightway cast out to woe and suffering. O gluttony, well ought we to complain of thee! Oh, if a man wist how many maladies follow from gluttonous excess, sitting at his table, he would be the more temperate of his diet. Alas! short throat and delicate mouth causeth—east and west and south and north, in earth, in air, in water—that men must grunt and sweat to get dainty meat and drink for a glutton! Well canst thou treat, O Paul, of this matter. "Meat unto belly and belly unto meat; God shall destroy both," as saith Paulus.

Alas! by my fay, it is a foul thing to speak this word and the act is fouler, when a man so drinketh of the white and red that of his throat he maketh a sewer through that cursed superfluity. The apostle, full sorrowful, saith, weeping, "There walk many of which I have told you, I say it now weeping with piteous voice, of which, sith they be enemies of the cross of Christ, the end is death; belly is their god." O paunch! O belly! O vile sack! how great labour and cost is it to provide for thee! These cooks, how they stamp and strain and grind and turn substance into accident to fulfil all thy luxurious desire. Out of hard bones they knock the marrow, for they cast naught away that may go through the gullet soft and sweet. For the glutton's pleasure, his sauce shall be made of spicery, of leaf and bark and root to whet him a new appetite. But certes he that resorteth to such delights is dead while he liveth in those vices.

A lustful thing is wine, and drunkenness is full of striving and misery. O drunken man, disfigured is thy countenance, sour is thy breath, foul art thou to embrace, and the sound through thy drunken nose seemeth as though thou aye saidest, "Samsoun, Samsoun," and yet Samson, God wot, drank never wine. Thou fallest as it were a stuck hog. Thy tongue is lost and all thy heed of honour, for drunkenness is the very sepulchre of man's discretion and wit. He in whom drink hath domination in very truth can keep no counsel. Now keep you from the white and the red, especially from the white wine of Lepe, that is for sale in Cheapside or Fish Street. This wine of Spain creepeth subtly into other wines growing near, of which such fumosity ariseth that when a man hath drunken three draughts and weeneth he be at home in Cheapside, he is in Spain, not at Rochelle or at Bordeaux, but right at the town of Lepe, and then he will say, "Samsoun, Samsoun."

But, lordings, I beseech you hearken one word, that all of the sovereign acts of victory in the Old Testament I dare say were done through God himself, that is all-powerful, in abstinence and prayer. Look in the Bible and there ye may learn it. Lo! Attila, the great conqueror, died shamefully in his sleep, bleeding aye at his nose in drunkenness. A captain should live soberly. And more than this, consider with diligence what was commanded to Lamuel—not Samuel, I say, but Lamuel; read the Bible and find it expressly set down concerning wine-giving to them that have the administering of justice. No more of this, for it is sufficient.

And now that I have spoken of gluttony, I will forbid you hazardry. Hazard is the very mother of lies and deceit and cursed forswearings, blasphemy of Christ, manslaughter and also waste of wealth and of time; and furthermore it is a reproach and dishonourable to be held a common gambler. And ever the higher he is of estate the more abandoned do men deem him.

If a prince pursueth hazardry, he is by common judgment held the less in reputation in any matter of policy or governance. Stilbon, a wise embassador, was sent in great pomp to Corinth from Lacedæmon to make an alliance with them. And when he came, it happened that he found all the greatest of that land playing at hazard. For which, as soon as might be, he stole home again to his own land and said, "There I will not lose my name, nor will I take upon me dishonour so great as to ally you unto gamblers. Send other wise embassadors, for by my truth I would liefer be dead than ally you with gamblers, for with such ye, that be so glorious in honour, shall not ally you, by my will or treaty." Thus said this wise philosopher. Witness eke, as the book saith, on the king of Parthia that sent in scorn to the king Demetrius a pair of golden dice, for before that he had practised hazard, and for the sake of it he held his glory or fame at no value or estimation. Lords may find other honourable kinds of pastime enow to drive time away.

Now I will speak a word or two of false and great oaths, as old books discourse on them. Great swearing is an abominable thing, and false swearing is yet more blameworthy. The high God forbade swearing at all; witness on Matthew, but in especial the holy Jeremy saith of swearing, "Thou shalt say thine oaths sooth and not lie, and swear in judgment and eke in righteousness." But idle swearing is cursed sin. Behold in the first table of high God's glorious commandments how his second behest is this: "Take not my name in vain." Lo! he forbiddeth such swearing earlier than homicide or than many a cursed thing. I say that in order it standeth thus; this know they that know his behests, how that this is the second behest of God. And furthermore I will tell thee flat that vengeance shall not depart from the house of him that is too outrageous of his oaths. "By God's precious heart and cross, by the blood of Christ that is in the abbey at Hailes, seven is my chance, thine is cinque and trey! By God's arms, if thou play falsely this dagger shall go through thy heart." This is the fruit that cometh of the two spotted dice-bones: ire, forswearing, homicide, falseness. Now for love of Christ that died for us, leave your oaths, both small and great. But now, sirs, I will tell forth my tale.

These three revellers of whom I speak, long ere any bell had rung for prime, had set them down to their cups in a tavern; and as they sat, they heard a bell clink before a corpse that was being carried to his grave. Thereat one of them gan call to the inn-boy, "Off with thee," quoth he, "and ask what corpse this is that passes by; and look thou report his name aright."

"Sir," quoth this boy, "it needeth never a whit to ask. It was told me two hours ere ye came here. Pardee, he was an old fellow of yours; and he was slain to-night of a sudden, dead drunk, as he sat on a bench. There came a stealthy thief—men call him Death—that slayeth all the people in this countryside, and he smote him with his spear through the heart, and went his way without more words. He hath slain, in this pestilence, a thousand; and master, ere ye come before him, methinketh it were needful for to beware of such an adversary. 'Be ready for to meet him ever and aye.' Thus my dame taught me; I say no more."

"By Saint Marie!" said the tavern-keeper, "the child saith sooth, for he hath slain this year, a mile hence in a great village, both man and woman, child, page and hind. I trow his habitation be there. To be wary were great wisdom in a man, lest this Death do him a dishonour."

"Yea, God's arms!" quoth the reveller, "is it then such peril for to meet him? I make a-vow to God's noble bones, I shall seek him highway and by-way. Hark, fellows; we three be of one mind. Let each of us hold up his hand and let us become sworn brethren among ourselves and we will slay this false traitor Death. He that slayeth so many—by God's dignity!— he shall be slain, ere it be night."

So together these three have plighted their troths to live and die for one another like brethren born, and in this rage, up they start all drunk, and forth they go toward that village of which the tavern-keeper had spoken, and with many a grisly oath have they rended Christ's blessed body, and sworn that Death shall be dead, if they may catch him.

When now they had gone half a mile or less, there met with them—right as they were about to step over a stile—an old poor man. This old man greeted them full meekly and said thus: "Now, lords, God you save." The proudest of these three revellers answered, "What, churl! The devil take thee! Why art thou all muffled save thy face? Why livest thou so long in great age?"

The old man looked him in the face and said thus: "Because I cannot find a man, yea though I walked to India, neither in town nor in city, that would exchange his youth for mine age. And therefore I must still keep mine age, for as long time as it is God's will. Neither will Death alas! neither will he have my life. Thus walk I like a restless caitiff; and on the ground, which is my mother's gate, both morn and eve I knock with my staff, and say: 'Dear mother, let me in! See how I wither, flesh and skin and blood. Alas! when shall my bones be at peace? Mother, I would exchange my chest with you, that hath been in my cham-

109

ber long time; yea, even for a shroud of hair-cloth to wrap me.' Yet she will not do me that favour; wherefore my face is so pale and withered. But, sirs, it is not courtesy in you to speak in churlish wise to an old man, unless he have trespassed in word or act. Ye may yourselves read in holy writ: 'In presence of an old man, whose head is hoar, ye shall arise.' Wherefore I counsel you do unto an old man no harm now more than ye would that men did to you in your old age, if ye tarry so long in this life. God be with you, whether ye walk or ride. Now must I go whither I have to go."

"Nay, old churl, that shalt thou not, by God!" answered then the second gambler. "By Saint John! thou partest not so lightly. Thou spakest right now of that traitor Death, that slayeth all our friends in these parts. By my troth, as thou art his spy, tell us where he is, or thou shalt rue it, by God and the holy sacrament! For soothly thou art leagued with him to slay us young folk, thou false thief."

"Now, sirs," quoth he, "if you would so fain find Death, turn up this crooked path, for by my fay I left him in yonder grove under a tree and there he will tarry; nay, not even for your boast will he hide himself. See ye that oak? Right there ye shall find him. God, that redeemed mankind, save you and amend you!"

Thus spake this old man. And all the revellers hasted till they came to that tree and there they found—coined in fine round gold—well nigh an eight bushel, as seemed to them, of florins. No longer then they sought after Death, for the florins were so bright and fair to see, and each was so glad of the sight, that down they sat by the precious hoard. The worst of them he spake the first: "Brethren," quoth he, "hearken what I say. Though I jest and make merry, yet my wisdom is great. This treasure hath fortune given unto us, to live our lives in jollity and mirth, and as lightly as it cometh so will we spend it. Eh, God's precious dignity! who had weened to-day that we should have so fair a grace? But now if this gold were but carried home to my house— or, if ye like, to yours—for well ye wot all this gold is ours, then were we in high felicity. But truly it may not be by day. Men would say that we were sturdy thieves, and would have us hanged for our own treasure. Nay, this treasure must be carried by night as wisely and as slily as may be. Wherefore I counsel that we draw cuts amongst us, and let see where the cut will fall; and he that draweth the cut shall run with blithe heart— and that full fast—to the town, and bring us bread and wine by stealth; and two of us shall guard this treasure craftily and well; and if he tarry not we will, when it is night, carry this treasure wheresoever with one consent it seemeth best to us."

Thereat one of them brought the cuts held in his fist, and bade them draw and watch where the cut would fall; and it fell upon the youngest; and forth he went anon towards the town. And even as soon as he was gone, the one of them spake thus to his fellow:

"Thou knowest well that thou art my brother, and I will tell thee somewhat to thy profit. Thou wotst well that our fellow is gone; and here is gold, and that a great sum, that shall be divided amongst us three. Natheless if I could so contrive that it were divided betwixt us two, had I not done thee a friendly turn?"

The other answered: "I wot not how that may be; he wot how that we twain have the gold. What shall we do? What shall we say to him?"

"Shall it be secret?" said the first rogue. "I will tell thee then in few words what we shall do, and I will bring it about."

"I make thee my vow," quoth the other, "by my truth, that I will not betray thee."

"Now," quoth the first, "thou wotst well that we be twain, and two of us shall be stronger than one. Watch when he shall be set down, and right anon rise up as though thou wouldst scuffle with him; and whiles that thou strugglest with him as in sport, I shall rive him through his two sides, and thou, with thy dagger, look thou do the same; and then shall all this gold be divided, my dear friend, betwixt me and thee. Then may we both fulfil all our pleasures, and play at dice right as we list." And thus be these two rogues accorded to slay the third, as ye have heard me tell.

The youngest—he that went to the village—full oft he rolleth up and down in his heart the beauty of those bright, new florins. "O Lord," quoth he, "if so I might have all this treasure to myself, there is no man that liveth under the throne of God should live so merry as I!" And at last the fiend, our foe, put it into his thought that he should buy poison, with which to slay his two companions. For the fiend had found him in such bad living that he had leave to bring him to perdition; for this rogue's design was utterly this, to slay his fellows both and never to repent.

No longer then he delayeth, but forth he goeth into the town unto an apothecary, and prayed him that he would sell him poison wherewith he might kill his rats; and eke in his yard there was a polecat, that (as he said) had slaughtered his capons; and fain, if he might, would he avenge him on the vermin that despoiled him by night. The apothecary answered: "Here thou shalt have a thing, and so may God save my soul! there is never a creature in all this world that shall eat or drink of this mixture, even the amount of a corn of wheat, but he shall yield up his life anon. Yea, die he shall, and that in less time than thou wilt go a mile at a walk; so strong and so violent is this poison."

This cursed reveller hath taken into his hand the poison in a box; and thereupon he ran unto a man in the next street and borrowed of him three large bottles; and into two poured he his poison. The third he kept clean for his own drink; for all that night he planned to toil in carrying away of the gold from that place. And when this reveller, sorrow betide him—had filled his three great bottles with wine, he repaireth to his fellows.

What needeth to discourse more of this? For even as they had devised his death at the first, right so have they slain him and that speedily.

And when this was done, thus spake one of them: "Now let us sit and drink and make joy, and afterward we will bury his body." And with that word it happed him perchance that he took the bottle wherein the poison was, and drank of it and gave his fellow also to drink, for which right anon they died both the two.

But certes I suppose that Avicenna wrote never in any canon or any chapter more wondrous signs of empoisoning than had these two wretches before their end.

Thus be ended these two homicides and eke the false empoisoner.

O cursed sin, full of cursedness! O wickedness! O traitor's homicide! O gluttony, lust and gambling! O thou blasphemer of Christ, with churlish tongue and monstrous oaths born of evil usage and pride! Alas, mankind! how may it befall that to thy Creator who made thee and bought thee with his precious heart's blood, thou art so unkind and so false, alas!

Now, good men, God forgive you your trespasses and keep you from the sin of avarice. Mine holy pardon may heal you all, if so be ye offer nobles, or sterlings, or else silver brooches, rings or spoons. Bow your heads under this holy bull! Here anon in my roll I enter your name. Into heaven's bliss shall ye go! You that will offer I will absolve by my high power as clean and pure as ye were born. Come up, ye wives! offer ye of your wool.—Lo, sirs, such is my sermon; and may Jesu Christ, that is our soul's leech, grant you his pardon, for that is best, I will not deceive you.

But, sirs, one word that I forgot in my tale. Here in my bag I have relics and pardons as fair as hath any man in England, which were given me by the pope's own hand. If any of you will offer with devoutness and have my absolution, come forth anon and kneel here, and meekly receive my pardon; or else take your pardons as ye ride all new and fresh at every town's end; but look that ye alway offer anew nobles and pence that be sound and good. To every wight that is here it is an honour that ye may have a pardoner sufficient to assoil you, in what-soever adventure may befall you in the country as ye ride. Per-chance one or two may fall down from his horse and break his neck in two. Look what a security it is for all of you that I am fallen into your fellowship to assoil you high and low, when the soul shall pass from the body. I counsel that our host here shall be the first, for he is most enveloped in sin. Come forth now, sir host, and offer first, and thou shalt kiss the relics, yea each and all, for a groat. Unbuckle thy wallet."

"Nay, nay," quoth he, "may I have Christ's curse if I do! Let be; I will not, say I. Thou wouldst make me kiss thine old hosen, and swear that they were the relics of a saint, were they never so filthy."

This pardoner was so wroth that he answered never a word.

"Now," quoth our host, "I will sport no longer with thee, nor with none other angry man." But right anon, when he saw that all the people laughed, spake the worthy Knight: "No more of this, for it is enough. Sir Pardoner, be glad and look merry. And ye, sir host, that be dear to me, I pray you that ye kiss the Pardoner. And Pardoner, I pray thee draw nearer, and let us laugh and sport as we did before." Anon they kissed and rode their way.

Here is ended the Pardoner's Tale.

The Wife of Bath's Prologue

The Prologue of the Wife's Tale of Bath.

"EXPERIENCE, though no authority were in this world thereon, were enough for me to speak of woe that is in marriage; for, lordings, since I was twelve years old, thanks be to God that liveth eternally, I have had husbands five at church-door, for so oft have I been wedded; and in their degree all were worthy men. But in sooth it was told me not long ago that, sith Christ went never but once to a wedding in Cana of Galilee, by the same ensample he taught me that I should be wedded but once. Lo! hark what a sharp word eke on this matter spake Jesus, man and God, beside a well in reproof of the Samaritan: 'Thou hast had five husbands,' quoth he, 'and that man which hath thee now is not thy husband;' thus said he in truth; what he meant thereby I cannot say; but this I ask: Why was the fifth man no husband to the Samaritan? How many might she have in marriage? Never yet in my life heard I a clear explication concerning this number. Men may conjecture and gloss it up and down, but well I wot, in very truth, that God bade us expressly to wax and multiply. That gentle text I can well understand. Eke I wot well he said mine husband should leave father and mother and take me; but of no number made he mention, whether of bigamy or of octogamy; why should men speak reproach of such?

"Lo, Dan Solomon! the wise king; I trow he had more wives than one, as would God I had leave to be refreshed half so oft as he! What a gift of God he had in all his wives! No man hath such now in this world. God be praised that I have wedded five, from whom I have plucked their best. Diverse schools make perfect clerks; diverse practice, in many sundry labours, maketh the workman thoroughly perfect; of five husbands am I the scholar. Welcome the sixth, whensoever he shall come. In sooth, I will not for aye keep me chaste. When mine husband is departed from the world, some Christian man shall wed me anon; for then, the apostle saith, I am free to wed, in God's name, where I list. It is no sin, he saith, to be wedded; better is it to be wedded than to burn. What reck I though folk speak reproach of accursed Lamech and his bigamy. I wot well Abraham was an holy man, and Jacob eke as far as I know; and each of them had wives more than twain, and many another holy man also. When saw ye ever that high God at any time expressly forbade marriage? I pray you tell; or where hath he commanded virginity? I wot as well as ye, in sooth, that the apostle, when he spake of maidenhood, said that precept thereof he had none. A man may counsel a woman to be a maid; but counselling is no command; he left it to our own discretion. For had God commanded maidenhood, then by that act had he damned marrying; and certes if there were sown no seed, whereof, then, should virginity grow? Even Paul durst not command a thing for which his master gave no precept. The prize is set up for virginity; let him win who may; let see who runneth best. But this word need not be received of every wight, but only where God list, of his power, to grant it. I wot well the apostle was a maid, but natheless, though he wrote that he would every wight were such as himself, all that is but counsel to virginity; and he gave me leave of his indulgence to be a wife; so it is no reproof to wed, if my mate be dead, without the charge of bigamy. This is the sum and substance: He held maidenhood more perfect than wedding in frailty; and frailty I call it, if the man and maid will not lead all their life in continence.

"I grant, in sooth, I reck not though maidenhood be preferred to bigamy; it pleaseth such to be clean, body and spirit; of mine own estate I will make no boast. For well ye know a lord in his house hath not every vessel of pure gold; some be of wood and do their lord service. God calleth folk to him in sundry ways, and each hath of God his own gift, some this, some that, as it pleaseth God to bestow. Virginity is a great virtue, and continence eke, with religious folk. But Christ, that is the spring of perfection, bade not every wight that he should go sell all he hath, and give it to the poor, and in such wise follow him and his steps. He spake but to them that would live perfectly, and by your leave, lordings, I am not such. I will bestow the flower of my life in the acts and in the fruit of marriage. But I say not that men should have no care of chastity. Christ was a maid, and yet created perfect man, and many a saint, since the beginning of the world, yet they lived alway in perfect chastity. I will envy no virgins; let them be bread of pure wheat-seed; and let us wives be called barley-bread; yet with barley-bread, as Mark telleth, our lord Jesu refreshed many a man. I will persevere in such estate as God hath called us to; I am not over-nice. An husband I will have, I will not forego him, that shall be my debtor and eke my thrall, and have his tribulation therewith while I am his wife. Whilst I live, I, and not he, shall have sway over him. Right thus was it told me by the apostle, that bade our husbands to love us well. That text pleaseth me every whit——"

Upstarted the Pardoner and that straightway; "Now, dame," quoth he, "by God and Saint John, ye be on this text a noble preacher. I was about to wed a wife. Alas! Why should I pay for it so dearly upon my flesh? Liefer had I wed no wife this year!"

"Abide!" quoth she, "my tale is yet to begin; nay, thou shalt drink of another tun, ere I go, shall savour worse than ale. And when I have told thee forth my story of tribulation in marriage, in which all my life I have been expert, that is to say, myself I have been the whip,—then mayst thou choose whether thou wilt taste of that tun which I shall broach. Beware of it, ere thou draw too nigh; for I shall tell ensamples more than twice five. Whosoever will not beware by others, by him shall others be corrected. The same words writeth Ptolemy; read in his Almageste and there find it."

"Dame, I would pray you, if it be your will," said this Pardoner, "as ye began, tell forth your tale, spare for no wight, and teach us young men of your practice."

"Gladly," quoth she, "sith it may please you. But yet I pray unto all this fellowship, if I speak after my fantasy, take not amiss what I say, for mine intent is but to sport. Now, sirs, will I tell forth my story. As ever I hope to drink wine or ale, I shall say the sooth; those husbands that were mine, three of them were good and two were bad. The three were good, rich and old. They had given me their goods and their treasure; I needed no longer take pains to win their love, or do reverence to them. They loved me so well, by heaven's king, that I set no value on their love! A wise woman will ever busy her to get love where she hath none. But sith I had them wholly in hand, and sith they had given me all their goods, why should I take pains to please them, unless it were for mine own profit and my pleasure? The bacon, I ween, was not fetched for them, that some men get at Dunmowe in Essex. I governed them after my law so well that each of them was full blissful and fain to bring me gay things from the fair. They were full glad when I spake to them well for, God wot, I chid them pitilessly.

"Now hearken how I bare me, ye wise wives that can understand. Thus shall ye speak and beguile them, for there can no man swear and lie half so boldly as a woman. I say not this concerning wives that be wise, unless it be when they have forgotten themselves. A wise wife, if she knoweth her own good, shall make him believe the chough is mad, and take her own maid to witness. But hark how I would speak.

"Sir, old dotard, is this thy treatment of me? Why is my neighbour's wife so gay? She is honoured wheresoever she goeth; I sit at home, I have no gown that I can wear. What dost thou at my neighbour's house? Is she so fair? Art thou so enamoured? What whisper ye with our maid? *Ben'cite!* Sir old rake, let be thy wiles. And if I have a friend or a gossip without guilt, thou chidest as a fiend, if I amuse me by going unto his lodging! Thou comest home as drunk as a mouse, and preachest on thy bench, bad luck to thee! Thou sayest to me it is a great misfortune to wed a poor woman for the cost thereof; and if she be rich, of high birth, then sayest thou that it is a torment to suffer her pride and her humours. And if she be fair, thou very knave, thou sayest that every rake will have her; she may no while remain in chastity that is assailed upon each side. Thou sayest some folk desire us for wealth, some for our shape and some for our fairness, and some because we can sing or dance, and some for gentility and playfulness, some for our hands and our slender arms; thus by thy tale goeth all to the devil. Thou sayest a castle-wall may be so long assailed on every side that men may no longer keep it. And if she be foul thou sayest that she coveteth every man she may see; for as a spaniel she will leap on him, till she find some man to bargain with her; and no goose so gray, sayest thou, goeth there in the lake as will be without a mate. And sayest it is a hard thing for to control a thing that no man will hold willingly. Thus sayest thou, old knave, when thou goest to bed. And that no wise man needeth to marry, nor any man that aspireth unto heaven; with wild thunder-clap and fiery lightning may thy withered neck be broken! Thou sayest that leaking roofs, and smoke, and chiding wives make men flee out of their own house. Ah! what aileth such an old man, *ben'cite!* to chide? Thou sayest, we wives will conceal our vices till we be fast wedded, and then we will show them; that may well be a rogue's proverb! Thou sayest that oxen, asses, horses and hounds at diverse times be tested; and so be basins and wash-pails, pots, clothes and other goods, spoons and tools, and all such chattels, ere men buy them; but of wives folk make no assay till they be wedded; and then, sayest thou, old dotard rogue, we will show our vices.

"Thou sayest also that it displeaseth me unless thou wilt praise my beauty, and pore alway on my countenance, and in every place call me 'fair dame;' and unless thou make a festival on my birthday, and make me gay and fresh of garb, and unless thou do respect to my nurse, and to my maidservant within my bower, and to my father's folk and his kindred;—thus thou sayest, old barrel full of lies!

"And yet of Jankin, our apprentice, for his crisp hair, shining as fine gold, and because he squireth me hither and thither, thou hast caught a false suspicion; I would naught of him, though thou wert dead to-morrow. But tell me this, why in the fiend's name hidest thou the keys of thy chest away from me? Pardee, my good is it as well as thine. Why weenest thou to make an idiot of thy lady? Now by that lord that is called Saint James, though thou be mad, thou shalt not be master both of my body and of my goods; one thou shalt forego, maugre thine eyes. What need hast thou to inquire of me, and spy upon me? I trow, thou wouldst lock me in thy chest! Thou shouldst say, 'Wife, go where it liketh you, take your disport, I will not believe any gossip; I know you for a true wife, dame Alis.' We love no man that taketh heed where we go; we would be free.

"May he be blessed of all men, the wise astrologer Dan Ptolemy, that saith in his Almageste this proverb: 'Of all men his wisdom is the highest that recketh never who hath the world in his hand.' This proverb thou shalt construe thus: if thou have enough, why needest thou reck or heed how merrily other folk fare? For certainly by your leave, old dotard, ye shall have right enough of your due in good time. He is too great a niggard that will refuse a man leave to light a candle at his lantern; he shall have never the less light, pardee; if so thou hast enough, thou needest not to complain.

"Thou sayest eke, if we make us gay with clothing and pre-cious gear, that it is peril unto our chastity; and yet more, sorrow betide thee! thou must enforce thy speech, and say these words of the apostle, 'In habit made with chastity and shamefastness, ye women shall apparel you, and not in tressed hair and gay jewels, as pearls, nor with gold, nor rich clothes.' In accordance with this text and rubric of thine, I will not perform as much as a fly. Thou saidest I was like a cat; for if a man will singe a cat's skin, then will the cat alway abide in his house; but if the cat's skin be sleek and fair, she will not dwell in house half a day, but ere any daylight be dawned, she will forth to show her skin and go a-caterwauling. This is to say if I be clad fair, sir rogue, I am running out to show my duds.

"Sir old fool, what aileth thee to spy upon me? Though thou pray unto Argus, with his hundred eyes, to be my body-guard as best he knoweth, in faith, he shall not keep me unless I please; still could I cozen him, on my life. Thou saidest eke that there be three things which trouble all this world, and that no wight may endure the fourth.—O sweet sir rogue, Jesu shorten thy days!—Yet thou preachest and sayest a hateful wife is reckoned for one of these mischiefs. Be there no other manner of resemblances that ye may use in your parables, unless a poor wife be one of them? Thou likenest woman's love to hell, to barren land, where no water may abide. Thou likenest it also to wild fire; the more it burneth, the more it hath appetite to consume everything that may be burnt. Thou sayest that even as worms ruin a tree, right so a wife destroyeth her husband; this know they that be bound to wives.

"Lordings, right thus stiffly, as ye have heard, I made mine old husbands believe that they had said thus when they were drunk; and all was false, but I took Jankin to witness and also my niece. O lord, the sorrow I made them and the woe, full guiltless, by God's sweet pain! For I could whine and bite as an horse. I could complain though I were in the guilt, or else oftentimes had I been lost. He that first cometh to mill grindeth first; I complained first, so I ended our strife. They were full glad to pray forgiveness full soon for things of which they were never guilty in their lives. I would accuse my husband of wenches when scarce he might stand for sickness. Yet it tickled his heart, for he weened that I had so great fondness for him. I swore that all my walking out by night was to spy on wenches that he wooed. Under colour of that had I many a mirth. For all such wit is given us when we are born. Deceit, weeping and spinning God hath given to women by nature while they live. And thus I vaunt me of one thing; in the end I had alway the better of them, either by sleight, or force, or by some manner of means, such as continual murmuring or grumbling. Especially would I chide and do them no pleasance, till they had made over their ransom to me. And therefore to every man I say this, let him win who may; for all is to sell. With empty hand men may lure no hawks. Though the pope had sat beside them, I would not spare them at their own table; I quit them word for word, by my troth. So help me very God almighty, though right now I should make my testament, I owe them no word that is not paid. I brought it so about by my wit, that they must give up, or else had we never been at peace. For though they looked as angry lions, yet should they fail of their end.

"Then would I say, 'Sweet love, give heed how meekly looketh Wilkin our sheep; come nearer, my spouse, let me kiss thy cheek! Ye should be all mild and patient and have a sweet, scrupulous conscience, sith ye so preach of Job. Be patient alway, sith ye can preach so well; and unless ye be, certainly ye shall learn how fair a thing it is to live with a wife in peace. Questionless one of us two must bow, and sith a man is more reasonable than woman is, ye must be the one to submit. What aileth you thus to grumble and groan? By God, ye be to blame; I say you the sooth.' Such manner of words had we together. Now will I speak of my fourth husband. My fourth husband was a reveller; that is, he had a paramour; and I was young and full of wild spirit, stubborn and strong and merry as a magpie. Well could I dance to a small harp, and sing, sooth, as any nightingale, when I had drunk a draught of sweet wine. Metellius, the foul churl, the hog, that slew his wife with a staff because she drank wine,—had I been his wife, he should not have daunted me from drinking; and after wine, I think most on Venus. In a vinolent woman there is no denial; this rakes know by experience. But lord! when I take remembrance upon my youth and my jollity, it tickleth me about the root of mine heart. Unto this day it doth mine heart good that I have had my world in my time. But alas! age, that will envenom all, hath bereft me of my pith and my beauty; let go, farewell, the devil go with them! The flour is gone, there is nothing more to say; the bran now I must bestow as best I am able. But yet will I endeavour to be right merry. Now will I tell of my fourth husband.

"I say, I had great despite in my heart that he had joy of any other. But I paid him, by God and Saint Bennet! I made him a cross of the same wood; not in any foul manner, but certainly I made folk such cheer that I made him fry in his own grease, for very anger and jealousy. God's name! I was his purgatory on earth, for which I hope his soul be in bliss. For God wot, he sat full oft and sang when his shoe wrung him full bitterly. No wight, save God and him, knew how sore, in many wise, I tormented him. He died when I came from

Jerusalem; under the rood-beam he lieth buried, although his tomb is not so curiously wrought as was the sepulchre of Darius, which Apelles wrought subtly; to bury him preciously were but waste. Let him fare well, God give peace to his soul; he is now in the grave and in his chest.

"Now will I speak of my fifth husband, God let his soul never come in hell! And yet he was the most rascally to me, as I feel on my ribs all in a row, and shall ever unto mine ending-hour. But he was so fresh and gay, and therewith he could so well cajole me, that though he had beat me in every bone, he could straightway win my love again. I trow I loved him best because he was sparing of his love to me. To speak sooth, we women have in this matter a quaint fantasy; is there a thing that we may not lightly have? thereafter will we cry ever and crave. Forbid us a thing, and we desire it; press on us hard, and then we will flee. We grudge to spread out all our goods; great press at market maketh dear wares; and too cheap is held at little worth; every woman that is wise knoweth this.

"My fifth husband, God bless his soul! whom I took for love and not for riches, was sometime a clerk of Oxford, and had left school, and went home to board with my gossip, that dwells in our town, God have her soul! Alisoun was her name. She knew mine heart and my privity better than our parish priest, as I live! I confided to her all my secrets. For had my husband done a thing that should have cost him his head, I would have told every whit of his secret to her and another worthy wife and to my niece, that I loved well. And so I did, God knoweth, full often, so that it made his face red and hot for very shame, and he blamed himself that he had told to me so great a privity.

"And so it befell that once, in Lent (I visited my gossip so often, for ever I have loved to be merry, and to walk, in March, April and May, from house to house, and hear sundry tales), that Jankin the clerk, and my gossip dame Alis, and I myself, walked into the fields. All that Lent my husband was at London; I had the better leisure to sport, and to see and eke to be seen of lusty folk; how wist I where my luck was destined to be? Therefore I made my visits to vigils and to processions, to preaching and eke to these pilgrimages, to plays of miracles, and weddings, and wore my gay scarlet skirts. These worms, nor these moths, nor these mites, ate them never a whit; and wotst thou why? for they were used well.

"Now will I tell forth what happened to me. I say that we walked in the fields, till verily we had such dalliance, this clerk and I, that I spake to him, and said to him, of my foresight, how if I were a widow, he should wed me. For certainly, I say it not for any boast, I was never yet without provision for marriage, nor for other things also. I hold that mouse hath a heart not worth a leek, which hath but one hole to start to, and if that fail, then is all lost. I made him believe he had enchanted me; my dame taught me that trick. And I said eke that I dreamed of him all night; he would have slain me, I dreamed, as I lay, and my bed was all full of very blood; but yet I hoped that he should do well by me, for to dream of blood betokeneth gold, I was taught. And all was false, I dreamed of it never at all, but I ever followed my dame's lore in this as in other things. But sir, let me see now, what shall I say? Aha! by Saint John! I have my tale again.

"When my fourth husband was on his bier, I wept aye and made a sorrowful face, as wives must, for it is custom, and with my kerchief covered my visage; but because I was provided with a new mate, I wept but small and that I warrant. My husband was borne to church in the morning by neighbours that made great sorrow for him; and Jankin our clerk was one of them. So God help me, when I saw him walking after the bier, methought he had a pair of legs and of feet so fair and clean, that I gave unto him all mine heart. He was twenty winter old, I trow, and if I shall not lie, I was forty; but yet I had alway a colt's tooth. Gap-toothed I was, and that well became me; I had the print of Saint Venus' seal. So God help me, I was fair and rich, a lusty one, young and joyous. For certes in feeling I am all Venerian, and mine heart is Martian. Venus gave me my jollity and my wantonness, and Mars my sturdy hardihood. Mine ascendent was Taurus, and Mars in it. Alas! alas! that ever love was sin! I followed aye mine inclination by virtue of my stars; this caused that the Venus in me could never resist a good fellow. Yet I have Mars' mark upon my face, for, so God save me! I never loved by discretion, but ever followed my desire, were he white or black, or short or long; so he pleased me, I recked not how poor he was, nor of what estate.

"What should I say but that, at the month's end, this jolly clerk Jankin, that was so courteous, wedded me with great joy and feasting, and to him I gave all the land and fee that had ever been given me; but I repented me afterward full sore. He would let nothing be to my liking. By God, he smote me once on the ear, because I rent a leaf out of his book, so that of the stroke mine ear waxed stone deaf.

"I was as stubborn as a lioness, and a very jangler with my tongue, and I would walk from house to house, as I had done before, even if he had forbidden it. For which oftentimes he would preach to me, and tell me of old Roman stories, how Simplicius Gallus left his wife, and forsook her as long as he lived, for naught but that he saw her upon a day looking out at his door bareheaded. Another Roman he told me of that forsook his wife eke, because she was at a summer's game without his knowing. And then would he seek in his Bible that proverb of Ecclesiasticus, where in his commandment he strongly forbiddeth a man to suffer his wife go gadding about; then ye may be sure he would say right thus:

'Whoso that buildeth all his house of sallows,
Whoso that spurreth his blind horse over the fallows,
And suffereth his wife seek shrines and hallows,
Is worthy to be hanged on the gallows.'

"But it was all for naught, I recked not a berry for his proverbs nor his old saws, nor would I be corrected of him. I hate him that telleth me my vices, and so do more of us than I, God wot! This made him utterly angry with me; I would not spare him in any case.

"Now by Saint Thomas, I will tell you the sooth why I rent a page out of his book, for which he smote me deaf. He had a book that gladly for his disport he would aye read day and night. He called it Valerie and Theofraste, at which book he laughed alway full merrily. And eke there was once a clerk at Rome, a cardinal, he was called Saint Jerome, that composed a book against Jovinian; in which book there were Crisippus, Trotula, Tertulan and Helowys, that was an abbess not far from Paris; and the Parables of Solomon, Ovid's Art and many a book, and all these were bound in one volume, and every night and day, when he had leisure and vacation from other worldly business, it was his custom to read on this book of wicked wives. He knew more legends of them and histories than there be of good wives in the Bible. For trust well, it is an impossibility that any clerk will speak good of wives, unless it be of holy saints, but of any other woman never. Who painted the lion, tell me who? By God, if women had written stories, as clerks have within their cells, they would have written of men more wickedness than the whole race of Adam might amend. The children of Mercury be full adverse in their working to those of Venus. Mercury loveth wisdom and knowledge, and Venus loveth riot and spending. And because of their diverse temperament, each declineth in the other's exaltation; and thus Mercury, God wot, is desolate in Pisces, where Venus is exalted; and Venus falleth where Mercury is uplifted; therefore no woman is praised of a clerk. The clerk, when he is old and hath lost his amorousness, then sitteth he down and writeth in his dotage that women cannot keep their wedding-vows!

"But now to my point, pardee, why, as I was about to tell thee, I was beaten for a book. On a night, my lord and master Jankin, as he sat by the fire, read on his book first of Eve, by whose wickedness all mankind was brought to woe, for which Jesu Christ himself was slain, and redeemed us with his heart's blood. Lo! here may ye see it expressly written of woman, that she was the perdition of all mankind. Then he read me how, when Samson lay sleeping, his mistress cut off his hair with her shears; through which treason he lost both his eyes. Then he read me of Hercules and his Deianira, that caused him to burn to death. Nor forgot he the penance and woe that Socrates had with his two wives; how Xantippe cast slops on his head; this poor man sat still, as one sleeping; he wiped his head and durst say no more than 'ere thunder stinteth cometh a rain.' The tale of Pasiphaë, that was queen of Crete, savoured to him pleasantly for her wickedness; fie! speak no more of her horrible lust and love; it is a grisly thing. Of Clytemnestra, that, for her wantonness, made her husband to die, he read it with full good devotion. He told me eke for what cause Amphiaraus died at Thebes; he had a legend of his wife, Eriphile, that for a clasp of gold privily revealed unto the Greeks the place where her husband hid him, for which he had a sorrowful fate at Thebes. Of Lyma he told me, and of Lucy, that both caused their husbands' deaths, the one for love, the other for hatred. Lyma, late on an even, poisoned her husband, because she had grown to be his foe. Lucy wantonly so loved her husband that, to make him alway have her in mind, she gave him such a manner of love-drink that he died, ere it was morrow; and thus husbands ever have woe.

"Then he told me how one Latumius complained to Arrius, his fellow, that a certain tree grew in his garden on which, he said, his three wives hanged themselves for anger of heart. 'O sweet brother,' quoth this Arrius, 'give me a graft of that blessed tree and it shall be planted in my garden!' He read me of wives of later date, how some slew their husbands in their beds. Some have driven nails in their husbands' brains while they slept, and thus they have killed them; some have given poison to them in their drink. He spake more harm than heart can conceive. And therewith he knew of more proverbs than there grow blades of grass in this world. 'Better is it,' quoth he, 'that thy habitation be with a lion or a foul dragon than with a woman that useth to chide. Better is it,' quoth he, 'to dwell high upon the roof than with an angry wife down in the house; they be so wicked and contrary, they hate aye what their husbands love.' He said, 'A woman casteth her shame away when she casteth off her smock,' and eke 'A fair woman, unless she be also chaste, is like a gold ring in a sow's nose.' Who can ween or conceive the woe and pain that was in my heart?

"And when I saw he would never have done all night reading on this cursed book, all suddenly I plucked three leaves out of his book, right as he read, and anon I so took him with my fist on the cheek that he fell down backward into our fire. And he started up as doth a mad lion, and so smote me with his fist on the temple that I lay on the floor as I were dead. And when he saw how still I lay, he was aghast and would have fled, till at last I started out of my swoon. 'O! hast thou slain me, false thief?' I said, 'and hast thou murdered me thus for my land? Yet ere I die, would I kiss thee.' And he came nigh and kneeled down gently and said, 'Dear sister Alisoun, so help me God, I shall never smite thee again; what I have done, thyself art to blame for. Forgive it me, I beseech thee.' And yet straight again I hit him on the cheek and said, 'Thief, thus mickle am I avenged; now will I die, I may speak no longer.' But at last, with mickle care and woe, we were accorded between ourselves. He gave me into my hand all the bridle to have governance of house and acres, and of his tongue and his hand also; and I made him burn his book then and there. And when, by my victory, I had got unto me all the power of governance, and he said, 'Mine own true wife, do as it liketh thee as long as thou shalt live, guard thine own honour and mine estate eke'—after that day we had never strife. So help me God, I was as loving to him as any wife from

Denmark to Ind, and as true, and so was he to me. I pray to God that sitteth in splendour to bless his soul, of his dear mercy. Now, if ye will hark, I will tell my tale."

Behold the words between the Summoner and the Friar.

The Friar laughed when he had hearkened to all this. "Now dame," quoth he, "as I hope for joy, this is a full long preamble of a tale!" And when the Summoner heard the Friar sing out, "Lo!" quoth he, "God's two arms! A friar will evermore be meddling. Lo, good men! a fly and a friar will fall in every dish and every affair. Why speakest thou of preambulation? What! amble, or trot, or stand still, or go sit down; thou hinderest our sport in this manner."

"Yea!" quoth the Friar, "wilt thou so, Sir Summoner? Now by my faith, ere I go, I shall tell such a tale or two of a summoner, that all the folk here shall laugh." "Now, Friar," quoth this Summoner, "I beshrew else thy face, and I beshrew myself, but I tell tales two or three of friars, ere I arrive at Sidingborne, as shall irk thine heart full sore, for well I wot thy patience is gone."

Our host cried, "Peace! and that straightway! let the woman tell her story," he said. "Ye fare as folk that be drunken with ale. Pray, dame, tell your story, and that is best." "All ready, sir, right as it pleaseth you," quoth she, "if I have permission of this worthy Friar." "Yes," quoth he, "tell forth, dame, and I will listen."

Here endeth the Wife of Bath her Prologue.

The Tale of the Wife of Bath

Here beginneth the Tale of the Wife of Bath.

IN the old days of King Arthur, of which Britons tell wondrous tales, all this land was filled with troops of fairies. The elf-queen danced full oft with her jolly company in many a green mead. This, as I understand, was the old opinion; I speak of many hundred years ago; for now no man can see any elves more. For now the prayers and the great charity of limiters and other holy friars that search every land and stream, as thick as motes in the sun's ray, blessing halls, chambers, kitchens, bowers, cities, boroughs, castles, high bastions, thorps, barns, dairies, stables,—this maketh that there be no fays. For where was wont to walk a fairy, there now, of afternoons and of mornings, walketh the limiter himself, and saith his matins and holy prayers as he goeth in his limit. Women may go safely back and forth, under every tree and bush; there is no other incubus but him and he will do them no dishonour.

It so befell that this King Arthur had in his house a knight, lusty and young, that on a day came riding from the river, and it happed that he saw, walking before him, a maid, alone as she was born, whom anon, despite her utmost, he bereft of her maidenhood, for which oppression there was such outcry and such complaint unto King Arthur, that this knight by course of law was condemned to die, and would peradventure have lost his head, such then was the statute, had not the queen and other ladies so long prayed the king of his grace, that he granted him instead his life, and gave him wholly to the queen, to choose at her will whether she would save or destroy him.

The queen thanketh the king with all her heart, and after when she saw her time, she spake thus to the knight: "Thou standest yet in such estate that thou hast no surety of thy life. I grant thee life, if thou canst tell me what thing women most desire. Be ware, and keep thy neck-bone from iron. And if thou canst not tell it at once, yet will I give thee leave to go for a twelve-month and a day, to seek and learn an answer sufficient unto this matter. And ere thou go, I will have surety that thou wilt yield up thy body in this place."

Woful is this knight and sigheth sorrowfully, but what! he may not do all things as he liketh, and at last he chooseth to depart and come again at the year's end with such answer as God would provide for him, and taketh his leave and wendeth forth on his way.

He seeketh every house and place where he hopeth, with heaven's favour, to learn what thing women love most, but in no region could he arrive where he might find two creatures agreeing together in this matter. Some said women love best riches, some said honour; some, mirth; some, rich raiment; some, marriage joys and to be ofttimes wed and widowed. Some said that our hearts be most content when we be flattered and pleased. I will confess, such cometh full nigh the sooth; a man shall best win us with flattery; and by attentions and petty courtesies we be snared, both more and less. And some say how we love best to be free and do even as we please, and to have no man reprove us of our vices, but say that we are wise and in no way foolish.

For truly if a wight will claw us on our sore place, there is none of us that will not kick, because he telleth us the truth; essay, and he that doth shall find it so; for be we never so vicious within, we would be held prudent and blameless. And some say that we take great delight to be thought staid and trusty with secrets, and steadfast in one purpose, and not communicative of things that men tell us; but that tale is not worth a rake-handle; pardee, we women can hide nothing; witness Mydas; will ye hear the tale?

Ovid, amongst other small things, saith that Mydas, under the long locks growing on his head, had two ass's ears, which blemish he hid, as best he could, full subtly from every man's sight, so that none other save his wife wist thereof. He loved her most and trusted her also. He prayed her that she should tell no creature of his disfigurement. She swore to him "nay," for all this world she would not commit such a sin and disgrace as to make her husband have so foul a reputation; she would not tell it for her own shame. Natheless it seemed to her that she would die if she must hold a secret so long; it seemed her heart swelled so sore that some word must needs start from her, and sith she durst tell it to no wight, down she ran to a marsh near by; her heart burned till she came there, and as a bittern bumbleth in the mire, she laid her mouth unto the water: "Betray me not, thou water," quoth she, "with thy sound; unto thee I tell it and none other; my husband hath long ass's ears twain! Now is my heart whole; now it is out; to save me I might no longer keep it." Here ye may see, though we may keep a secret for a time, yet it must out, we cannot hide it.

This knight, of whom my tale is especially, when he saw that he could not come at what women love most, was full sorrowful at heart and in spirit; but home he goeth, he might not tarry. The day was come when he must turn homeward; and on his way, in all this woe, it happed that he rode under a forest-side, where he saw going upon the dance more than four and twenty ladies, toward whom he drew rein full eagerly, in the hope that he might learn some wisdom. But certain is it, that ere he reached this dance, it was vanished, he wist not where. No living creature he saw, save that on the green he saw a wife sitting; a fouler wight no man can imagine. This old wife gan rise up to meet the knight and said: "Sir Knight, here lieth no path. Tell me, by your fay, what ye seek? Peradventure it may be the better for you. We old folk know many things." "My good mother," quoth this knight truly, "I am no better than dead, unless I can say what thing women most desire. Could ye inform me, I would requite you well."

"Plight me here thy troth in my hand," quoth she, "that thou wilt do the next thing that I require of thee, if it lie in thy power, and ere night I will tell it you." "Have here my troth," quoth he, "I consent."

"Then," quoth she, "I dare pledge thy life is safe, for I will stand by it, on my life, the queen will say as I. Let see which of them that is proudest and weareth a head-kerchief, or a caul, dare say nay to that which I shall teach thee. Let us go forth without more talk." Then she whispered a sentence in his ear, and bade him be glad and have no dread.

When they were come to the court, this knight said that he had kept his day, as he had sworn, and his answer was ready. Full many a noble wife and maid, and many a widow, for they be wise, were assembled—the queen herself sitting as a judge— to hearken his answer; and soon this knight was bade to appear.

Unto every wight was commanded silence, and unto the knight that he should tell in open court what thing worldly women love best. This knight stood not still as a dumb brute, but to his question straightway answered with manly voice, so that all the court heard it. "My liege lady," quoth he, "universally woman desireth to have dominion both over her husband and his love, and to have mastery over him. This is your utmost desire, though ye kill me. Do as ye list, I am here at your mercy."

In all the court there was nor maiden, nor wife, nor widow, that denied what he said, but they said he was worthy to live. At that word up started the old wife, whom the knight saw sitting on the green. "Pardon," quoth she, "my sovereign lady! Ere your court depart, do me justice. I taught this answer unto the knight, for which he plighted me his troth, that he would do the next thing I should require of him, if it lay in his power. Before the court, then, I pray thee, Sir Knight, that thou take me to wife; for well thou wottest that I have saved thee. If I speak false, say nay, on thy faith!"

This knight answered: "Alas! welaway! I wot right well that such was my promise. For God's love, choose a new request; take all my wealth, but leave my body."

"Nay then," quoth she, "beshrew us both! for though I be foul and old and poor, I would not for all the metal and gold, which is buried under earth, or lieth upon it, that I were other than thy wife and eke thy love." "My love? Nay," quoth he, "my damnation! Alas! that any of my race should ever be so foully disgraced!" But all was for naught; the end is, that he was constrained to espouse her; and he taketh his old wife and goeth to bed.

Peradventure now some folk will say that in my negligence

I take no pains to tell you the joy and all the ordinance of the feast that day; to which I shall briefly answer. There was no joy nor feast at all; there was only heaviness and much sorrow; for he wedded her on a morning privily, and afterward hid himself all day as an owl, so woful was he that his wife looked so loathsome. Great woe had the knight in his heart when he was brought abed with his wife; he rolleth from side to side and turneth to and fro. His old wife evermore lay smiling and said, "O dear husband, *ben'cite!* fareth every knight thus with his wife? Is this the law of King Arthur's house? Is every knight of his so unapproachable? I am your own love and eke your wife; I am she which hath saved you; and certes never yet did I wrong unto you; why fare ye thus with me this first night? Ye fare like a man that hath lost his wit; what is my guilt? for God's love, tell me, and if I can, it shall be amended."

"Amended? Alas!" quoth this knight, "nay, nay! It will never be amended more! Thou art so loathsome and so old, and come eke of so low a birth, that little wonder it is, though I wallow and wind. Would to God my heart would burst!" "Is this," quoth she, "the cause of your restlessness?" "Yea, certainly," quoth he, "and no wonder." "Now, sir," quoth she, "ere three days' space, if I list, I could amend all this, so that ye might bear you well unto me. But sith ye speak of such gentleness as is descended from ancient wealth, wherefore ye say ye should be accounted gentle, such arrogance is not worth a hen. Look to him who, privily and openly, is alway most virtuous, and ever inclineth most to do the gentle deeds he is able, and take him for the greatest gentleman. Christ desireth that we claim from him our gentleness, not from our ancestors because of their ancient wealth. For though they may give us all their heritage, for which we claim to be of high birth, yet in no wise may they bequeath to any of us their virtuous living which made them to be called gentlemen; and Christ bade us follow them in that respect.

"Well can the wise poet of Florence, Dante, speak in this regard; lo! in such verse is Dante's tale:

> 'Full seldom upward into the small branches
> Riseth the worth of man; for God desireth
> That we should claim from Him our gentleness.'

For of our ancestors we may claim nothing but temporal things, which men may hurt and harm. Every wight eke wot this as well as I, that if gentleness were planted by nature in a certain lineage, then would they of that line cease never, privily or openly, to do the fair offices of gentleness; they could do no discourtesy or sin.

"Take fire, and bear it into the darkest house betwixt Mount Caucasus and here, and let men shut the doors and go thence; yet will the fire blaze and burn as fair as though twenty thousand men might behold it; on my life, it will perform its natural office till it die.

"Here may ye see well how gentility is not tied down to possession, sith folk perform not their proper functions alway as doth lo! the fire after its kind. For, God wot, men may full often see a lord's son do shame and dishonour. And he that would have praise for his gentility, because he was born of a gentle house, and had ancestors virtuous and noble, and will do no gentle deeds himself, nor imitate his gentle ancestor, he is not gentle, be he a duke or a prince; for rude, sinful deeds make a churl. For gentleness which is but the renown of thine ancestors for their high worth is a thing strange to thine own person; thy gentleness cometh to thee from God alone; true gentleness, then, cometh unto us by grace; it was in no wise bequeathed us with our birth.

"Think how noble was that Tullius Hostilius, that rose—as saith Valerius—out of poverty unto high nobility. Read Seneca and read eke Boethius; there shall ye see expressed without doubt that he is gentle who performeth gentle deeds; and therefore, dear husband, I draw to an end thus, that although mine ancestors were rude, yet may the high God, as I hope, grant me grace to live virtuously. Then shall I be gentle, when I live virtuously and eschew sin.

"And whereas ye reprove me of poverty, the high God, on whom we believe, chose of his own will to live in poverty. And certes every man, maid, or wife, may understand that Jesus, heaven's king, would not choose a vicious life. Glad poverty, sooth, is a seemly thing; this Seneca saith, and other clerks. Whosoever considereth himself paid of his own poverty, I hold him rich, though he have not a shirt. He that coveteth is a poor wight, for he would have that which is not in his power. But he that hath naught, nor coveteth to have, is rich, though ye may consider him but a hind. True poverty singeth of its own nature; Juvenal saith pleasantly of poverty: 'The poor man, when he goeth by the way, may sing and sport before the thieves.' Poverty is a gift hateful to its possessor, but as I ween, a great remover of cares; a full great repairer eke of wisdom to him that taketh it in patience, and although it seem wretched, it is a possession no wight will calumniate. Full oft, when a man is humble, poverty maketh him to know his God and eke himself.

Poverty methinketh is a glass, through which he may see his true friends. And therefore, sir, sith I vex you naught, reprove me no more of my poverty.

"Now, sir, ye reprove me because of mine old age; and certes, sir, though there were no authority thereon in any book, yet ye honourable gentles say that men should show favour unto an old wight, and of your gentleness call him father; and I ween I shall find authorities.

"Whereas, too, ye say that I am foul and old, therefore dread not that I shall be false to thee; for, as I live, filth and old age be great wardens of chastity. Natheless sith I know your pleasure, I shall fulfil your worldly desire. Choose now one of these two things, to have me foul and old till I die and be to you a true, humble wife and never displease you in all my days, or else to have me young and comely, and take your chances of the resort that shall be to your house, because of me, or perchance to some other place. Now choose yourself, whichever it liketh you."

This knight taketh counsel with himself and sigheth sore, and at last he saith in this manner: "My lady and my love and my dear wife, I put me in your wise governance; choose yourself which may be most pleasure and most honour to you and eke to me; I reck not to which of the two; for as it liketh you it sufficeth me." "Then," quoth she, "have I got the mastery of you, sith I may choose, and govern as it liketh me?" "Yea, certes, wife," quoth he, "I deem it best." "Kiss me," quoth she, "let us be wrathful no longer, for by my word, I will be both to you, that is to say, both fair, yea, and good. I pray to God that I may die mad unless I be to you as good and faithful as ever wife was since the world was new; and unless I be to-morrow as fair to see as any lady, empress or queen that is betwixt the east and the west, do with me in life and death as it liketh you. Cast up the curtain and look how it is."

And when the knight saw verily that she was so fair and eke so young, for joy he caught her in his two arms, his heart bathed in a bath of bliss. A thousand times in succession he gan kiss her; and she obeyed him in everything, that might do him pleasure or gladness. And thus they live all their lives in perfect joy; and Jesu Christ send us husbands meek, young and lusty, and grace to outlive them that we wed. And eke I pray Jesu to shorten their days that will not be governed by their wives; and unto old and angry niggards God send soon a very pestilence.

Here endeth the Wife's Tale of Bath.

The Clerk's Prologue

"SIR CLERK of Oxford," said our host, "ye ride as shy and still as a maid newly wedded and sitting at the board. I have heard never a sound from your tongue this day. I trow ye study about some sophism; but Solomon saith: 'Every thing hath its time.' For God's sake be of better cheer; this is no time to ponder. Tell us some merry tale, by your faith; for the man that is entered into a game he needs must agree unto the terms of the game. But preach not as friars do in Lent, to make us weep for our old sins, nor so as to put us to sleep with thy tale. Tell us some merry thing of adventures. Your terms, your colours and your figures of logic keep them in store till so be ye may endite in high style, as when men write to kings. Speak at this time I pray you so plain that we may understand what ye say."

This worthy clerk answered courteously: "Host," quoth he, "I am under your rod; ye have the governance of us at this time, and therefore will I render you obedience as far, certainly, as reason asketh. I will tell you a tale which I learned at Padua from a worthy clerk, as his words and his work have proved him. He is dead now and nailed in his chest. I pray God give peace to his soul!

"Francis Petrarch was the name of this clerk, the laureate poet whose sweet rhetoric illumined all Italy with poetry, as Linian did with philosophy or law or some other special art. But death, that will not suffer us to dwell here but, as it were, the

So much of Dalliance
and fair Speech ✠ · ✠ · ✠

twinkling of an eye, hath slain both of them; in like wise must he slay all of us.

"But to tell forth as I began of this worthy clerk that taught me this tale, I say that first ere he writeth the body of his tale he enditeth with high style a proem, in the which he describeth Pemond and the country of Saluces and speaketh of Apennine, the high hills that be the bounds of west Lombardy; and in special of Mount Vesulus, where from a small spring the Po taketh its rise and source, ever increasing in its flow eastward toward Emelia, Ferrare and Venice. All of which were a long thing to describe. And truly, in my judgment, methinketh it an impertinent thing, save that he wisheth to introduce his subject. But this is his tale, which ye may hear."

The Clerk's Tale

Here beginneth the Tale of the Clerk of Oxford.

ON the west side of Italy, at the foot of Vesulus the cold, there is a lusty plain abounding in all good cheer, where thou mayst view many a tower and town that were founded in the time of our forefathers, and many another delectable sight, and Saluces was the name of this noble country. A marquis was whilom lord of it, as were his worthy elders before him, and all his lieges were obedient and ready to his hand, both low and high. Thus he liveth in delight and hath done long, beloved and dreaded, through fortune's favour, both of his lords and of his commons. Of lineage he was eke the gentlest born in Lombardy, fair of person, strong, young, and full of courtesy and of honour; discreet enough to govern his country, save in some matters wherein he was at fault; and Walter was this young lord's name. I blame him in this, that he considered not what might befall him in time to come, but all his thought was on present pleasure, as to hawk and hunt far and near; well nigh all other cares he let slide, and eke—what was worst of all— for naught that might hap, would he wed a wife. That one point his people bare so grievously that they went to him on a day in a flock, and one of them, because that he was the wisest of lore, or else that the marquis would most willingly hear him tell what the people thought, or else that he could discourse the best of such a thing,—he said to the marquis as ye shall hear:

"O noble marquis, as oft as there is need that we tell unto you our heaviness, your humanity giveth us assurance and courage. Permit now, lord, of your grace, that we lament unto you with piteous heart, and let not your ears disdain my voice. Although I have naught to do with this matter more than another man hath that is here, yet as ye, my dear lord, have alway showed me your grace and favour, I dare the better ask of you a little while of audience, to show our request, and do ye, my lord, even as it liketh you. For certes so pleasing to us be ye and all your work and ever have been, lord, that we could not ourselves devise how we might live in more felicity, save in one thing, lord, that, if it be your will, it might please you to be a wedded man; then were your people utterly in heart's content. Bow your neck under that blissful yoke of sovereignty, not of servitude, which men call spousal or wedlock; and think, lord, amongst your wise thoughts, how in sundry fashion our days pass, for though we sleep, or wake, roam or ride, time fleeth aye, it will wait for no man. And though as yet your green youth flowereth, in creepeth age alway, as still as a stone, and death menaceth young and old, and smiteth in each estate, for none escapeth; and as certain as we all know that we shall die, so uncertain be we all of that day when death shall betide us. Accept then the loyal meaning of us, that never yet refused your behest, and lord, if ye will assent, we will choose you a wife in short time, born of the gentlest and the highest of all this land, so that, as we believe, it ought to seem an honour to God and to you. Deliver us out of all this anxious fear, and wed a wife, for high God's sake; for if—as God forbid—it should so befall that through your death your lineage should cease, and a strange successor should take your heritage, oh, woe were us alive! Wherefore we pray you right soon to wed!"

Their meek prayer and their piteous look made the heart of the marquis to have pity. "Mine own people dear," quoth he, "ye would constrain me to what I never thought ere now. I rejoiced in my liberty; seldom is it found in marriage. Where till now I was free, I should enter into servitude. Natheless I see your loyal meaning and trust in your wit, and ever have done; wherefore of my free consent I will wed me, as soon as ever I may. Yet though ye have but now offered to choose me a wife, I release you of that choice, and pray you to stint of that offer. For God wot that children oft be unlike their worthy elders before them. Goodness cometh all of God, not of the strain of which they be engendered and born. I trust in God's goodness and therefore I commit to him my marriage and mine estate and my repose; he may do as he list. Let me alone in the choosing of my wife; that charge I will take upon mine own back. But I pray you, and charge you upon your souls, that whatsoever wife I take, ye promise me to honour her, while her life may endure, in word and work, here and everywhere, as she were an emperor's daughter. Furthermore ye shall swear this, that ye shall neither contend nor grumble against my choice; for sith I am to forego my liberty at your request, where my heart is set, there, as I hope for heaven, will I wive; and unless ye will assent to this, I pray you speak no more of the matter."

With hearty will, they swore and assented to all this; no wight said nay; and they besought him of his grace, ere they went that he would grant them a certain day for his espousal, as early as ever he could; for somewhat yet the people feared lest this marquis would wed no wife in spite of all.

He granted them such day as liked him, on which he would surely be wedded, and said he did this at their request; and they, with humble mind, all kneeling full reverently upon their knees, thanked him with all humility, and thus they were satisfied of their desire, and home they went again. Thereupon he commanded his officers to provide for the festival, and gave such charge to his household knights and squires as he list to lay upon them; and they obey his commandments; and each doth all his diligence that the nuptials might be splendid.

Part II

Not far from that lordly palace where this marquis purposed his marriage, stood a hamlet, pleasant of site, in which poor folk had their beasts and their abode, and took sustenance from their labour according as the earth gave them of its plenty. Amongst these poor folk dwelt a man that was held the very poorest; but high God can sometime send his grace into a little ox's-stall; Janicula was his name, and he had a daughter full fair to behold, and this young maiden was called Grisildis. But if men speak of the beauty of virtue, then was she one of the fairest under the sun, for she was fostered in poverty; no lustful pleasure had stirred her heart. Ofter of the well than of the cask she drank, and in obedience to virtue she knew much of labour but naught of idle ease. But though this maid was tender in years, yet in her virgin breast was enclosed a ripe and staid spirit; and with great reverence and love, she cherished her old, poor father.

While she watched her few sheep in the field, she would do her spinning; she would not be idle till she slept. And when she came homeward, she would cull ofttimes roots and herbs, which she shred and seethed for their living, and she made her bed full hard; and aye she sustained her father's life with all compliance and diligence that a child may perform to honour her father.

Upon this simple maid, Grisildis, the marquis full oft set his eye as haply he rode a-hunting; and when it chanced that he beheld her, he cast not his eyes upon her with wanton look of folly, but in serious wise he would oft peruse her face, commending her womanhood in his heart, and eke her virtue, surpassing any other of so young age, as well in look as in deed; for though the people have no great insight into virtue, he considered full well what men said of her goodness, and determined that he would wed her only, if ever he should wed.

The day of the wedding came, but no wight could tell what woman it should be; for which marvel many a man wondered and said, when he was in private, "Will not our lord leave his folly? Will he not wed? Alas, alas the time! Wherefore will he so beguile himself and us?" Natheless this marquis hath had rings made and brooches of gems, set in azure and gold, for Grisildis' sake; and he took the measure of her clothing by a maid like to her of height, and eke of all other adornments that pertain unto such a wedding.

The time of undern approacheth of the day when this wedding should betide, and all the palace was arrayed, both chambers and hall, each in its degree. There mayst thou behold servants' offices stuffed with abundance of daintiest victual that may be found as far as utmost Italy. This royal marquis, richly arrayed, in company with the young knights of his retinue, and the lords and ladies that were bidden unto the spousals, with sound of various melody and in festal wise, held the straight way unto the village of which I told. Grisildis, full innocent, God wot, that all this festivity was devised for her, is gone to fetch water at a well, and cometh home as fast as she may, for she had heard it said how that same morn the marquis should wed, and if she might, she fain would see some of that procession. She thought, "I will stand in our doorway, with other maidens that be my fellows, and see the marchioness, and therefore I will try, as soon as I may, to do my labour at home, and then at leisure I may behold her, if she take this way unto the castle." And as she stepped over her threshold, the marquis came and gan to call her, and anon she set down her water-pot beside the threshold in the stall of an ox, and down she fell on her knees, and kneeled still with serious countenance till she had heard what was the lord's wish.

The thoughtful marquis spake to this maid full soberly and said in this wise: "Where is your father, Grisilde?" And she, with reverence and humble mien, answered, "Lord, he is ready here." And she went in without longer tarrying, and fetched her father to the marquis. He took then this old man by the hand, and when he had led him aside, said thus: "Janicula, I cannot longer conceal the delight of my heart. If thou vouchesafe, whatsoever befall, I will, before I go, take thy daughter to my wife for as long as she shall live. Thou lovest me—I wot it well—and art my true liegeman born, and all that liketh me I dare to say liketh thee, and therefore tell me specially that point whereof I spoke even now, whether thou wilt consent to take me for thy son-in-law?"

These sudden tidings so astonished this man that he waxed red, abashed, and stood quaking; scarce could he speak and only these words: "Lord," quoth he, "my willing is as ye will, nor will I aught against your liking; ye be my dear lord; do in this matter right as ye list."

"Yet," quoth this marquis softly, "I desire that in thy chamber I, thou and she may have a conference, and wottest thou why? Because I would ask if it be her will to become my wife and govern herself after my desire; and all this shall be done in thy presence; I will speak naught out of thy hearing."

And while they were in the chamber about their covenant which ye shall hear afterward, the people came without the house, and marvelled how honourably and heedfully she kept her dear father. But Grisildis might well wonder without end, for never before saw she such a sight. It is no wonder she was astonished to see so great a guest enter there; never had she been accustomed to such guests; wherefore her face looked full pale. But briefly to pursue this story, these be the words that the marquis spoke to this true, faithful, gentle maid.

"Grisilde," he said, "ye shall understand well that it pleaseth your father and me that I wed you, and eke, as I suppose, it may well be that ye too will it so; but these questions I ask first, whether, sith it is done so hastily, ye will assent or else deliberate. I say this: be ye ready with good heart to perform all my pleasure, so that I may freely, as seemeth me best, cause you to laugh or to grieve; and do ye promise never, day or night to grumble? and eke when I say 'yea,' not to say 'nay,' neither by word nor by frowning countenance? Swear this, and here I swear our espousal."

Wondering at these words and quaking for fear, she said:

"Lord, unfit and unworthy am I for that honour which ye bid me; but as ye yourself will, even so will I. And I swear here that never willingly in act nor in thought will I disobey you; rather would I be dead, though I were loath to die." "This is enough, Grisilde mine," quoth he; and he goeth forth with full sober cheer out at the door, and she came after, and in this manner he spoke to the people: "This is my wife, that standeth here; let whosoever loveth me honour her, I pray, and love her; there is no more to tell you."

And that she should bring naught of her old gear into his house, he commanded women to unclothe her right there; whereat these ladies were not right glad to handle her clothes, which she wore. Natheless they have clothed this bright maid all new from head to foot. They combed her hair, that lay full rudely untressed, and with their slender fingers they set a crown upon her head, and adorned her with jewels, great and small; why should I make a tale of her array? The people scarce knew her for her beauty, when she was transfigured with such richness.

This marquis hath espoused her with a ring, brought for that purpose, and then set her upon a snow-white horse that ambled gently, and with joyful folk that accompanied and that came forth to meet them, conveyed her unto the palace, without longer tarrying; and thus they spent the day in revelry, till the sun gan sink. And briefly to pursue this tale, I say that God of his grace hath sent such favour unto this new marchioness, that it seemed not of likelihood that she was born and bred so rudely as in a cot or an ox-stall, but nourished in an emperor's palace. To every wight she waxed so dear and worshipful that the folk where she was born, who had known her year by year from her birth, scarce believed it was she, but durst have vowed that she was no daughter to Janicula; for it seemed to them she was another creature. For though she was ever virtuous, she increased in such excellence of virtues, set in noble graciousness, and was so discreet and fair of speech, so benign and so worthy of respect, and could so take unto herself the people's heart, that every wight loved her that looked on her face. Not only in Saluces was the goodness of her name published, but eke thereabout in many a region; if one spake well of her, another said the like; and the fame of her noble goodness so spread that men and women, both young and old, went to Saluces to look upon her.

Thus Walter lowly wedded (nay, royally, with honour and good fortune) liveth at home in happiness and the peace of God, and of outward blessings he had enough; and because he saw that virtue was oft hid under low degree, his folk held their lord a prudent man, and that is seen full seldom. This Grisildis understood not only the performance of womanly home-duties, but eke, when the case required, she could serve the public good; there was no discord, rancour, nor grief in all that land that she could not appease, and wisely bring all to rest and contentment. Though her husband were absent, and high folk or others of her country were wroth, she would reconcile them. Such wise and ripe words she had, and judgments of such equity, that men deemed she was sent from heaven to save people and to amend every wrong.

Not long after Grisildis was wedded, she bore a daughter, although she would liefer have borne a man-child. Thereof this marquis was glad, and eke the folk, for though a maid-child had come first, she might in likelihood attain unto a man-child, sith she was not barren.

THE CLERK'S TALE

Part III

It befell, as many times it befalleth, that when this child had been suckled but a short while, this marquis so longed in his heart to try his wife to learn her steadfastness, that he might not expel from his heart this strange desire; needlessly, God wot, he planned to affray her. He had tested her enough ere this and found her ever good; what needeth it for to tempt her ever more and more? Though some men praise it for subtle wit, as for me, I say that it ill fitteth a man to try his wife, and to put her in anguish and fear, when there is no need. To which end the marquis wrought in this manner: At night, where she was lying, he came alone, with stern face and look full troubled, and said thus: " Grisilde, that day in which I took you out of your poverty and put you in high noblesse, ye have not forgotten that, as I ween. I say, Grisilde, that this present dignity in which I have put you, maketh you not forgetful, I ween, in spite of any weal which ye may now have, that I took you in poor estate and full low. Give heed unto every word that I say to you; there is none that heareth it but we twain. Ye wot well yourself how ye came into this house, it is not long since, and though ye be pleasing and dear to me, ye be not so unto my gentles; they say it is great shame and woe unto them to be subjects and vassals of thee, that comest of a small village. And especially since thy daughter was born have they spoken these words; but I desire to live my life in rest and peace with them, as before; I may not, in this case, be unmoved by them; I must do with thy daughter for the best, not as I would but as it pleaseth my people. Yet full loath am I, God wot, to do this, and without your knowledge

I will not, but natheless this is my wish, that ye give me your consent unto this thing. Show now that patience which ye promised and sware unto me in your home that day when our marriage was made."

When she had heard all this, she changed not in word or look or countenance; she appeared not even grieved, but said, "Lord, all lieth in your pleasure; my child and I be yours all, with heart-felt obedience, and ye may save or destroy your own; do after your own will. So may God have my soul as nothing that pleaseth you may displease me; and I desire to have naught, and dread to lose naught, save only you. This will is in my heart, and shall ever be. Not death nor length of time may remove it, nor change me to another temper."

Glad was this marquis of her answer, yet he feigned as he were not so; all dreary was his look when he went out of the chamber; and ere long he hath privily told unto a man all his purpose, and sent him to his wife.

This trusty man was an officer of his whom oft he had proved faithful in great things, and to such folk eke things bad may be entrusted safely. The lord knew well that he loved and feared him; and when this officer wist the will of his lord, into the chamber he stalked, full quietly. "Madame," he said, "ye must forgive me though I do the thing to which I am constrained; ye be so wise that ye know full well the behests of a lord may not be shunned; they may well be lamented or bewailed, but a man must needs bow unto their pleasure; and so will I; there is no more to say. This child I am commanded to take"—and no more he spoke, but caught the child out of her arms all pitilessly and gan make as though he would slay it ere he departed. Grisildis must needs suffer all and consent; and as a lamb she sitteth quiet and meek and let this cruel officer perform his will. Ill-boding was the ill-fame of this man; ill-boding his face and eke his words, ill-boding the time in which he did this. Alas! her daughter whom she loved so—she weened he would have slain it right then. Natheless she neither wept nor sighed, consenting to what pleased the marquis. But at last she spake and meekly prayed the officer, by his worth and gentle blood, that she might kiss her little child ere it died. And with full sad face she laid it in her bosom and gan kiss it, and lulled it, and after blessed it. And thus she said in her gentle voice: "Farewell, my child, I shall see thee nevermore; but sith I have marked thee with the cross, blessed mayst thou be of that Father which died for us upon a cross of wood. Thy soul, little child, I commit to him, for this night for my sake shalt thou die."

I trow for a nurse it had been hard to see this piteous sight. Well then might a mother have cried "Alas!" Natheless she was so steadfast that she endured all the pain, and said meekly to the officer, "Have here again your little young maiden; go now and do my lord's bidding. But one thing of your grace will I pray you, that, unless my lord forbade you, ye at least bury this little body in some spot where no beasts nor birds may rend it." But he would speak no word in answer, and took the child and went his way.

This officer came again to his lord, and told him of Grisildis' words and look, point for point, and gave the child to him. Somewhat ruthful was this lord, but natheless he held to his purpose, as lords do when they will have their will; and he bade his officer that he should privily wind and wrap this child full soft with all tender care, and carry it in a coffer or in a blanket, but—on pain of losing his head—that no man should know of his purpose, nor whence he came nor whither he went; and that he should take it to his dear sister, at Bologna, who was countess of Panago, and make known to her this matter, and beseech her do her diligence to foster this child in all gentleness; and for aught that might befall, he bade her hide from every wight whose child it was.

The officer goeth and fulfilleth this thing; but now return we to this marquis, for now he imagineth full busily whether he might perceive by his wife's look, or by her words, that she was changed; but ever he found her alike steadfast and gentle. In every wise as glad, as humble she was, as busy in service and in love as she wont to be; nor of his daughter spake she a word. For all her pain, no strange look did she ever chance to show, nor ever named she her daughter's name, in earnest or in sport.

Part IV

In this wise there passed four years ere she was with child; but then, as God would, she bore a man-child by this Walter full gracious and fair to look upon; and when the folk told it to the father, not only he but all his country were merry for this child, and they thanked and praised God.

When it was two years old and taken from the breast of its nurse, this marquis on a day caught yet another whim to try his wife once again, if he might. O needless was she tried! But wedded men know no moderation when they find a patient creature. "Wife, ye have heard ere this," quoth the marquis, "how my people beareth ill our marriage, and especially now, since my son was born, it is worse than ever before; the murmuring slayeth my heart and my spirit, the complaint cometh so bitter to mine ears. Thus they say: 'When Walter is gone, then shall the blood of Janicle succeed and be our lord, for we have none other.' Such words, in truth, my people say; and good heed ought I to take of such murmuring, for certainly I dread such thoughts though they be not spoken plainly in my hearing. I will live in peace if I may; wherefore I am utterly determined to serve this child privily even as by night I served his sister. Of this I warn you that ye may not, on a sudden, go beside yourself for woe; be patient, thereof I pray you." "I have said," quoth she, "and shall ever say thus: I wish for nothing and I refuse nothing, save in sooth as ye list; it grieveth me not at all though my daughter and my son be slain, at your command that is to say. I have had no share of my two children save first sickness, and afterward pain and woe. Ye be our lord, do with your own things ever as ye list; ask no counsel of me. For as I left at home all my clothing when I first came to you, even so left I my will and all my freedom, and took your clothing; wherefore I pray you do your pleasure; I will obey your wish. And certes if I had prescience of your will ere ye tell it me, I would perform it without neglect; but now that I wot your desire, firmly and stably I receive it; for if I wist that my death would gladden you, right gladly would I die to please you. Death weigheth naught in comparison with your love." And when this marquis saw the constancy of his wife, he cast down his two eyes, and wondered how she could suffer all this grief in patience. And forth he goeth with a dreary countenance but unto his heart it was a full great delight.

This ugly officer, in the same wise as he took her daughter, even so, or worse (if men can imagine worse), hath snatched her son, that was full fair. And ever alike in the same manner she was so patient that she made no sign of sorrow, but kissed her son, and afterward marked him with the cross; and thereupon she prayed the officer that, if he might, he would bury her little son in the earth, to save his tender limbs, delicate to see, from birds and from beasts. But she could get no answer from him. He went his way, as though he recked not; but tenderly he brought the child to Bologna.

This marquis wondered at her patience ever more and more, and if he had not ere this known in sooth that she loved her children perfectly, he would have weened that of subtlety or malice or cruel mood she suffered this with unchanged visage. But truly he knew well that next himself she loved her children best of all; and now I would fain ask of women if these tests might not suffice? What more could a ruthless husband invent to test her wifehood and steadfastness, and he continuing ever in cruelty? But there be folk of such temper that, when they have conceived a certain purpose, they cannot stint of their intention, but even as if they were bound to a stake, they will not desist from that first purpose. Right so this marquis hath fully determined to try his wife, as at first he was disposed. He waiteth to see whether, by word or look, her heart had changed toward him, but never could he find variance; she was ever one in heart and visage; and aye the older she waxed, the more true to him, if that were possible, was she in love, and the more pains-taking. Whereby it thus seemed that there was but one will in them both; for as it pleased Walter, the same was also her pleasure; and God be thanked, all happed for the best. She showed well that a wife should not, for any disquiet that she may suffer, will anything save as her husband willeth.

THE CLERK'S TALE

The slander spread wide and oft concerning Walter that because he had wedded a poor woman, he had of cruel heart murdered privily both his children. Such murmuring was general among the people; no wonder, for no word came to their ears but that the children were murdered. So that, though his people before had loved him well, the slanderous report of his infamy made them to hate him. Murderer is an hateful name. Natheless for earnest nor for sport would he stint of his cruel purpose; all his thought was set to tempt his wife.

When his daughter was twelve years old, he sent to the court of Rome, that were privily informed of his will, a messenger, commanding them to frame such bulls as might suffice for his cruel purpose, declaring how the pope bade him, for his people's repose, to wed another, if he list. I say he bade them counterfeit the pope's bulls, declaring that he had leave by the pope's dispensation to put away his first wife, thereby to stint the rancour and dissention betwixt his people and him; thus said the bull, and they made it known at large. The rude people weened full well—and no wonder—that it was even thus. When these tidings came to Grisildis, I deem her heart was full of woe; but she, this humble creature, evermore constant, was ready to suffer all the adversity of fortune, attending ever his will and pleasure to whom, as to her very all in all in this world, she was given heart and soul. But, that I may tell this story shortly, this marquis hath written a private letter in which he sheweth his purpose, and hath sent it secretly to Bologna. Much he prayed the earl of Panago, who was wedded to his sister, to bring home again his two children, openly in honourable estate. But one thing he prayed him most, that he should tell no wight, though men should ask, whose children they were; but say that the maiden

161

should be wedded anon unto the marquis of Saluces. And as this earl was prayed, so he did; for on the day appointed he went forth toward Saluces, and many a lord eke in rich array, to escort this maiden and her young brother riding beside her. Arrayed full of bright gems was this fresh maid for her marriage; her brother, who was seven years old, arrayed eke full fresh as became his youth; and thus amid great noblesse and glad cheer, shaping their journey toward Saluces, they ride forth from day to day.

Part V

In the meanwhile, according to his wicked habit, in order to test his wife even further to the uttermost proof of her spirit, and fully to have knowledge and experience whether she were steadfast as formerly, this marquis on a day in open audience, spake to her full rudely these words: "Certes, Grisilde, I took great pleasure in wedding you for your goodness, your fidelity and your obedience, though not for your lineage or for your riches; but now that I consider it well, I know in very sooth that there is sundry and great servitude in the estate of a lord. I may not do as every ploughman; my people crieth out day after day and constraineth me to take another wife; and eke the pope, to assuage the rancour, giveth, I dare affirm, his consent thereto; and this much truly I will tell you, that my new wife is upon her way hither. Be strong of heart and straightway depart from her place, and take again that dower which ye brought me—I grant that of my favour— and return to your father's house. No man alway may have prosperity. Endure with even heart, I advise you, the strokes of fortune." And she answered again patiently, "My lord, I know and knew alway that betwixt your magnificence and my poverty no wight can make comparison; thereof is no doubt. I never deemed me in any manner worthy to be your wife, no, nor your chambermaid. And in this house where ye made me a lady—I take for my witness the high God, may he so surely comfort my soul!—I never held me lady nor mistress, but the humble servant of your worship, above every worldly creature, and that shall I ever, while my life may last. That ye of your goodness have held me so long in honour and noble estate where I was not worthy to be—for that I thank God and you, and to God I pray that it may be requited unto you; there is no more to say. Unto my father will I gladly depart and dwell with him unto my life's end. Where I was fostered a little child, there till I die will I lead my life—a widow clean in body, in heart and in all. For sith I gave unto you my maidenhood and am in sooth your faithful wife, God shield that I, the wife of such a lord, should take another man to husband and to mate. And God of his favour grant you weal and prosperity of your new wife, for I will gladly yield her my place, in which I was wont to be full blissful; for sith it pleaseth you that I shall go, my lord, that whilom wast all my heart's content, I will go when ye list. But though ye proffer me such dowry as I first brought, I have well in mind it was but my wretched clothes and uncomely, which it were hard now for me to light upon. O good God! how gentle and how kind ye seemed by your speech and your look the day that our marriage was made! But it is said truly—at least I find it so, for in me it is proved indeed—'love grown old is not as when it was new.' But certes, for no adversity, lord, even though it were death, shall it hap that ever I repent, in word or work, that I gave you my whole heart. My lord, ye wot that in my father's house ye caused me to be stripped of my poor garb, and clad me of your grace richly. Naught else I brought to you, in sooth, but faith and nakedness and maidenhood; and here I return again my clothing, and my wedding-ring forevermore. The rest of your jewels, I dare promise, be ready within your chamber. Naked I came forth of my father's house, and naked must I return. And yet I hope it be not your intent that I go smockless out of your palace. Ye could not do so dishonourable a thing as suffer that bosom, in which your children rested, to be seen all bare before the people in my walking; wherefore I beseech you, let me not go my way like a worm. Remember, my own dear lord, I was your wife, though unworthy. In guerdon of my maidenhood, therefore, which I brought hither but may not bear hence, vouchesafe to give me, as my meed, only such a smock as I was wont to wear, wherewith I may wrap the bosom of her that was your wife; and here I take my leave of you, my own lord, lest I trouble you more."

"The smock that thou hast on thy back," quoth he, "let it abide and bear it with thee." Yet scarce could he speak that word, but went his way for ruth and for pity. Before the folk she strippeth herself and in her smock, with head and foot bare, she is gone forth toward her father's house.

The folk, weeping, follow her along her way, and aye they curse fortune as they go; but she kept her eyes dry from weeping, nor at any time spake a word. Her father, that anon heard these tidings, curseth the day that nature framed him a living wight. For doubtless this old man had ever been suspicious of her marriage; for he deemed ever since it took place that when the lord had fulfilled his pleasure, he would think it disparagement to his estate to stoop so low, and would renounce her as soon as ever he might. Hastily he goeth toward his daughter, for by noise of the folk he knew of her coming, and as best he might he covered her with her old coat, full sorrowfully weeping; but he could not put it on her, for the cloth was rude and older by many a day than at her marriage.

Thus for a certain time dwelleth with her father this flower of wifely patience, in such wise that neither by her words nor her face, neither before the folk nor out of their sight, she showed that wrong had been done her, nor had she, by her countenance, any recollection of her high estate. No wonder is it, for in her noble estate her spirit ever was entirely humble. No tender mouth, no dainty desires, no pomp, no simulation of royalty, were hers; but she was full of patient gentleness, aye discreet, prideless, honourable, and ever to her husband steadfast and meek. Men speak of Job and most for his humility, as clerks when they list can write well, especially of men, but in soothfastness, though clerks praise women but little, there can no man acquit himself in humility as a woman can, nor can be half so faithful as women be, unless it hath befallen newly.

From Bologna is come this earl of Panago, the rumour of which spread among high and low, and in the ears of all the people it was made known that he had brought with him a new marchioness, in such pomp and wealth, that never before with human eyes was there seen so noble an array in West Lombardy.

The marquis, who knew and contrived all this, ere the earl was come, sent for that innocent poor Grisildis; and she, with humble spirit and glad visage, not with any swelling thoughts in her heart, came at his behest and fell on her knees and reverently and prudently greeted him. "Grisilde," quoth he, "my will is, that this maiden whom I shall wed be received to-morrow in my house as royally as is possible, and that every wight be honoured after his degree in his place at table, in attendance and in festal pleasure, as best I can devise. I have indeed no women capable of arraying the chambers in the manner which I would have; and I would fain, therefore, that all such governance were thine; thou knowest of old eke all my pleasure in such a thing. Though thine array be bad and ill to look upon, do at least thy duty." "Not only, my lord," quoth she, "am I glad to do this your pleasure, but I desire also to serve and please you according to my station, without fainting, and shall evermore; nor ever, for weal or woe, shall the spirit within my heart stint to love you best with all my true will."

And with that word she gan to prepare the house, to set the tables and make the beds, and took pains to do all in her might, praying the chambermaids for God's love to hasten, and busily shake and sweep; and she, the most serviceable amongst them, hath arrayed his hall and every chamber.

About undern gan alight this earl, that brought with him these two noble children, for which the people ran to gaze on their array, so richly were they beseen; and then folk begn to say among themselves that Walter was no fool, though it pleased him to change his wife, sith it was for the best. For, as they all deemed, she was fairer and more tender of age than Grisildis, and fairer fruit and more gracious should be bred of them, because of her high descent; her brother eke was so fair of face that the people took delight to see them, commending now the action of the marquis.

Auctor. "O stormy people! ever unstable and faithless! Aye undiscerning and changeful as a weather-cock, delighting ever in new rumours, for aye like the moon ye wax and wane, ever full of idle prating, not worth a farthing; your judgment is false, your constancy proveth naught; a full great fool is he that believeth in you."

Thus said serious folk in that city when the people gazed from high and low, glad for the mere novelty to have a new lady of their town. No more now will I speak of this, but to Grisildis again I will address myself, and tell of her constancy and her diligence.

Full busy was Grisildis in all that pertained to the feast. She was not abashed of her clothing, though it was rude and eke somewhat torn; but with glad cheer she is gone to the gate with the other folk to greet the marchioness, and after that busieth herself once more. With such glad cheer she receiveth her guests, and so properly, each after his rank, that no man discerneth a fault; but aye they wonder who she may be, that is clad in such poor array yet knoweth so much of ceremony, and full highly they praise her discretion. In the meanwhile she stinted not to commend this maid and eke her brother, with all her heart and full kindly, so well that no man could praise them better.

But at last, when these lords thought to sit down to meat, the marquis gan summon Grisildis, as she was busy in the hall.

"Grisilde," quoth he, as it were in sport, "how liketh thee my wife and her beauty?" "Right well, my lord," quoth she; "in good faith, I saw never a fairer. I pray God let her prosper; and even so I hope he will grant to you great joy unto the end of your life. One thing I beseech and eke warn you, that ye sting not with tormenting this tender maid, as ye have done unto

167

others; for she hath been more tenderly fostered, and in my belief she could not suffer adversity as could a poorly fostered creature."

And when Walter saw her fortitude and glad cheer and how she bare no malice, and that he so often had done offence to her, and she aye stable and constant as a wall, continuing her innocence ever throughout, this cruel marquis gan incline his heart to take pity upon her wifely steadfastness.

"This is enough, Grisilde mine; be now no more aghast nor sorrowful," quoth he. "I have assayed thy faith and thy goodness, in great estate and in lowly garb, as well as ever woman was tried. Now know I, dear wife, thy steadfastness." And he took her in his arms and gan kiss her. But for wonder she marked it not; she heard not what thing he said to her, but fared as she had started out of sleep, till she awaked out of her bewilderment. "Grisilde," quoth he, "by God that died for us, thou art my wife; I have none other, nor ever had, so God save me! This is thy daughter, that thou supposed to be my wife; that other, on my faith, as I have ever intended, shall be mine heir; verily thou borest him in thy body; at Bologna privily have I kept him. Take them to thee again, for now thou mayst not say that thou hast lost either of thy two children. And I warn well the folk that have said otherwise of me, that I have done this deed for no malice nor cruelty, but to test in thee thy womanhood, and not— God forbid!—to slay my children, but to keep them in quiet privily till I knew thy temper and all thy heart."

When she heareth this, she sinketh down in a swoon for piteous joy, and after her swoon she calleth both her young children unto her, and piteously weeping, embraceth them in her arms, and tenderly kissing them, full like a mother, with her salt tears she batheth both their hair and their visages. O how pitiful it was to see her swooning, and to hear her humble voice! "Grammercy, lord," quoth she, "I thank you that ye have saved me my children dear! Now I reck not though I die even now; sith I stand in your love and in your favour, death mattereth not, nor when my spirit may pass. O tender, O dear, O young children mine, your woful mother weened evermore that cruel hounds or foul vermin had eaten you; but God of his mercy and your gentle father have caused you tenderly to be kept," and in that same moment all suddenly she sank on the ground. And in her swoon so firmly she holdeth her two children in her caress, that only with great pains and skill could they release them from her arms. O many a tear ran down upon many a pitying face of them that stood near her; scarce could they abide about her. Walter maketh her glad and stinteth her sorrow. She riseth up abashed from her swoon, and every wight maketh joy and festivity unto her, till once more she hath in control her countenance. Walter so faithfully waiteth on her pleasure that it is rare to see the looks betwixt them both, now they be brought together again.

These ladies, when they saw their time, took her into a chamber and stripped her out of her rude array, and in cloth of gold that shone brightly, with a crown upon her head set with many a rich gem, they brought her into the hall, and there she was honoured as she was worthy to be.

Thus this piteous day had a blissful end, for every man and woman did his best to pass the time in mirth and revel, till starlight shone in the welkin; for more sumptuous was this feast in every man's sight, and greater of cost, than was the revel of her marriage.

Full many a prosperous year these two lived in concord and peace, and Walter married his daughter richly unto a lord, one of the worthiest of all Italy; and then in peace and content he sustained his wife's father in his court till the soul crept out of his body. The son of the marquis succeeded to his heritage in peace, after his father's day, and was fortunate eke in marriage, although he put not his wife to great trial. This world, it may not be denied, is not so strong as it was in old times; hearken therefore what this author saith.

This story is told not that wives should follow Grisildis in humility, for it were insupportable if they did; but that every wight, in his own estate, should be constant in adversity as Grisildis was; therefore Petrarch telleth this story, which he enditeth in high style. For sith a woman was so patient unto a mortal man, the more ought we to receive in good part all that God sendeth us; for with good reason he may assay that which he wrought. But though he tempteth no man whom he hath redeemed, as Saint James saith, if ye will read his epistle, yet he tryeth folk every day, there is no doubt; and suffereth us to be beaten in sundry wise with sharp scourges of adversity, not to know our hearts, for certes ere we were born he knew all our weakness, but for our discipline; and all his governance is for our best welfare. Let us live then in virtuous submission.

But, lordings, hearken one word ere I go: it were full hard to find nowadays Grisildes two or three in a whole town; for if they were put to such tests, the gold of them now hath such bad alloys of brass that though the coin be fair to the eye, it would break in two rather than bend. Wherefore now, for love of the Wife of Bath, whose life and all of her sect may God maintain in high mastery (else were it a pity!), I will, with lusty heart green and fresh, recite you a song to gladden you, I trow; and let us stint of earnest matter. Hearken my song, that saith in this wise.

Chaucer's Epilogue

Grisilde is dead and eke her patience,
    And both interr'd in far Italia's vale;
For which I cry in open audience
    Let no man be so hardy as to assail
The patience of his wife, in hope to find
    Grisildis', for so surely he shall fail.

O noble wives, ye sovereigns of sense,
    Suffer no lowliness your tongues to nail,
Nor any clerk have cause, or find pretence,
    To write of you so marvellous a tale
As of Grisilde long-suffering and kind,
    Lest Chichevache devour you, to your bale.

Ape Echo, that will own no diffidence
    But answereth ever up and down the dale;
Be not made fools of for your innocence,
    But sharply wield of governance the flail;
Imprint full well this lesson in your mind,
    For common profit, sith it may avail.

Ye archwives, stand alway on your defence,
    Sith as a camel ye be strong and hale,
And suffer men to do you none offence;
    Ye slender wives, that bend in battle's gale,
Be terrible as tigers yon in Ind;
    Aye clap as doth a mill-wheel, when ye rail.

171

Dread not mankind, do them no reverence,
    For though thy husband arméd be in mail,
The arrows of thy crabbéd eloquence
    Shall pierce his armour and his breast impale;
In jealousy I charge that thou him bind,
    And thou shalt make him couch as doth a quail.

If thou be fair, go forth where throngs be dense
    To show thy duds and face without a veil;
If thou be foul, be lavish of expense;
    To find thee lovers follow aye the trail;
Be aye of cheer as light as leaf i' the wind,
    And let him weep and wring his hands and wail!

Here endeth the Clerk of Oxford his Tale.

The Squire's Tale

"SQUIRE, come nearer if ye will and say somewhat of love; for certes ye know as much thereof as any man."

"Nay, sir," quoth he, "but I will say heartily as best I know how; for I will not revolt against your wish; I will tell a tale. If I speak amiss, have me excused. My will is good; and lo! this is my story."

Here beginneth the Squire's Tale.

AT Sarray, in Tartary, there dwelt a king, that warred against Russia, so that many a doughty man died. This noble king was called Cambinskan, and in his time was of so great renown that there was nowhere in any land so excellent a lord. He lacked naught that becometh a king. In the sect that he was born to, he obeyed his creed, as he was vowed, and thereto he was wise, hardy and rich, ever alike pious and just, true of his word, honourable and benign, of spirit steadfast as the earth, young, fresh and strong and in arms as ardent as any new-made knight of all his house. Of fair person he was, and prosperous, and kept alway such royal estate that there was nowhere such another as he. This noble king, Cambinskan, this Tartar, had on Elpheta, his queen, two sons, of whom the eldest was called Algarsyf, the other Cambalo. A daughter he had besides, that was the youngest and was named Canacee; but to tell you of all her beauty lieth not in my tongue nor in my cunning. I dare not attempt so high a matter; mine English is insufficient. He must be a surpassing rhetorician, that knoweth the colours belonging to his art, who should describe her every whit. I am none such; I must speak as I know how.

It so befell when this Cambinskan hath borne his diadem twenty winters, that he bade cry—as, I trow, was his yearly wont—the feast of his nativity throughout his city Sarray, on the last Ides of March when they came around. Full joyous and clear was Phœbus, the sun, for he was nigh his exaltation in Mars' face, and in his mansion in Aries, the sign hot and choleric. Full lusty was the weather and mild, so that the birds, against the bright sun, what with the season and the young green, sang full loud their affections. It seemed they had got them shields against the keen, cold sword of winter.

This Cambinskan, of whom I have spoken to you, with royal vestments and diadem sitteth full high on the dais in his palace, and holdeth his feast, so sumptuous and rich, that never in this world was one like to it. If I should tell the ordinance thereof it would occupy a summer's day; it needeth not eke to describe the order of their service at every course. I will not tell of their strange delicacies, nor of their swans, nor of their hernshaws. Besides, in that land, as old knights tell us, some food is held full dainty, which in this land men reck of but little. There is no man that may report all things. I will not delay you, for it is prime, and it should but waste the morning. Therefore I will turn again unto my first matter.

It so befell, after the third course, while this king sitteth thus among his noblesse, hearkening his minstrels deliciously play before him at the board, that all suddenly in at the hall-door came a knight on a steed of brass, and in his hand a broad mirror. On his thumb he had a ring of gold, and hanging by his side a naked sword, and up he rideth to the high board. In all the hall there was uttered no sound for marvel of this knight; but busily old and young gan stare on him. This strange knight that came thus on a sudden, all armed save his head full richly, saluteth king and queen and lords in their order as they sit in the hall, with such deep reverence and obeisance, in both speech and look, that Gawain, though he were come again out of Faërie, with his old courtesy, could not amend him with a word. And after this, before the high table, he saith his message with manly voice without defect of a syllable, after the form used in his language, and that his tale might the more please, as the art of speech teacheth them that learn it, his looks accorded with his words. Albeit I cannot express his style, nor climb over a stile so high, yet I say this: thus much to common understanding— if so be I have it rightly in mind—amounteth all that ever he spake.

He said: "My liege lord, the King of Araby and of Ind saluteth you on this festal day as best he can, and in honour of your feast, sendeth you by me, that am your servant, this steed of brass, that can easily, in the space of one natural day, that is to say, four and twenty hours, bear your body wheresoever ye list, without harm to you, in rain or shine, through fair or foul, into every place to which your heart willeth to go; or, if ye list to fly as high in the air as doth an eagle when he list to soar, this same steed shall bear you evermore without harm, though ye rest or sleep on his back, till ye be where ye list, and return again at the twirling of a pin. He that wrought it understood full many a device; he observed many a constellation ere he had done his work; and knew many a magic seal and full many a bond. Eke this mirror that I have here hath such a might that a man may behold in it when there shall befall any adversity unto your kingdom, or yourself, and openly who your friend is, or foe. And beside all this, if any fair lady hath set her heart on any manner of wight, if he be false, she shall see his treason, his new love and all his subtlety so openly, that nothing shall be hidden. Wherefore, against this lusty summer's tide, he hath sent this mirror and ring to my lady Canacee, your excellent daughter that is here.

"The virtue of the ring, if ye will learn, is this: that, if she list to wear it upon her thumb, or carry it in her purse, there is no fowl flieth under the heaven but she shall understand his voice and know plainly and openly his meaning, and answer him in his language. And she shall know eke every grass that groweth upon root, and to whom it will do cure, however deep and wide be his wounds. This naked sword, that hangeth beside me, hath such virtue that whatsoever man ye smite, it will cut and pierce clean through his armour, were it thick as a branched oak; and whatsoever man is wounded by the blow shall never be whole till ye list of grace to stroke him with the flat in the spot where he is hurt; that is to say, ye must stroke him again with the flat of the sword in the wound, and it will close; this is the very sooth, without lying; it faileth not while it is in your possession."

And when this knight hath thus told his tale, he rideth out of the hall and lighteth down. His steed, which glittered as the sun, standeth in the court, as still as marble. The knight is led anon to his chamber, and is unarmed and set at meat. The

There came a Knight
upon a Steed of Brass

Page 175

presents be fetched full royally, the mirror and sword, and borne anon by certain officers appointed thereto into the high tower; and unto Canacee, where she sitteth at the table, this ring is borne with ceremony. But in very sooth, the horse of brass may not be removed; it standeth as it were glued to the ground. No man may pull it out of the place, with any engine of windlass or pulley, and with good reason, for they know not the art. Therefore they have left it in the place till the knight hath taught them how to move it forth, as ye shall hear afterward.

Great was the press that to and fro swarmeth to gape on this horse where it standeth; for it was as high and as broad and long, and as well proportioned for strength, as if it were truly a steed of Lombardy; therewith it was as horsely and quick of eye, as if it were a noble Apulian courser. For certes, from his tail to his ear, not nature nor art could amend him in any degree, as all the people weened. But evermore they wondered most how it could go and was of brass. It was of Faërie, thought the people. Diverse folk deemed diversely. As many heads so many wits. They murmured like a swarm of bees, and made explanations according to their fancies, and said—rehearsing these old poetic fables—it was like the Pegasus, the horse that had wings to fly; or else it was the horse of Synon, the Greek, that brought destruction to Troy, as men may read in these old romances. "Mine heart," quoth one, "is aye afeard; I trow some men of arms be therein, that plan to capture this city. It were good that such things were known." Another whispered low to his neighbour and said: "He lieth; it is rather like an apparition made by some magic such as jugglers sport with at great feasts." Thus they talk and babble of sundry doubts, as unlearned people commonly deem of things that be made more subtly than they in their ignorance can understand. They be fain to construe a thing for the worse. And some of them wondered on the mirror, that was borne up into the chief tower of the castle, how men might see such things in it. Another answered and said it might well be caused naturally by compositions of angles and sly reflections, and said that there was such an one in Rome. They speak of Vitulon and Alocen and Aristotle, that wrote in their lifetimes of curious mirrors and perspective-glasses, as they know that have read their books. And others wondered on the sword that would pierce through all things; and gan to speak of King Thelophus, and of Achilles with his curious spear, for he could both heal and harm with it, even in such wise as men might with the sword of which ye right now have learned. They speak of sundry hardenings of metal, and therewith speak of certain drugs, and how and when it should be tempered, which is unknown at least unto me.

Then they speak of Canacee's ring, and all say that none of them had ever heard of such a wonder of ring-craft, save that Moses and King Solomon had a name for cunning in such a thing. Thus say the people and draw apart. But natheless some said it was likewise wonderful to make glass of fern-ashes; but because men have known it for so long, therefore ceaseth their babbling of it and their marvel; even as some marvel sore on the cause of thunder, on ebb and flood, gossamers, mist, and all things till the cause is known. Thus they deem and babble and imagine till the king riseth from the board.

Phœbus hath left the angle meridional, and the royal beast, the gentle Lion, with his Aldiran, was yet ascending, when this Tartar king rose from his board, where he sat aloft. Before him goeth the loud minstrelsy till he cometh to his chamber of rich hangings, where they play upon diverse instruments, that it is like an heaven to hear. Now dance the lusty children of Venus, for aloft in the Fish sitteth their lady and looketh on them with friendly eye.

This noble king, this Cambinskan, sitteth high in his throne; straightway this strange knight is fetched to him, and on the dance goeth with Canacee. Here is the revel and the jollity that a dull man cannot describe. He must have known Love and his service and been a festive man fresh as May, that should describe to you such a sight. Who could tell you the form of dances, such rare, fresh faces, such subtle lookings and dissimulatings for fear of the perceivings of jealous men? No man but Launcelot, and he is dead. Therefore I pass over all this merriment; I say no more, but leave them in this jollity till folk address them to the supper.

The steward biddeth the spices to be fetched in haste, and the wine eke in all this melody. The ushers and squires go and come anon with the spices and the wine; men eat and drink, and when this is done, as was reason, they wended unto the temple. The service done, they all sup by daylight. What needeth to rehearse to you the array upon the board? Every man wot well that at a king's feast is plenty for high and low, and more dainties than be in my knowledge. After supper this noble king goeth to see the horse of brass, with all the throng of lords and ladies about him.

Such wondering there was on this horse of brass that never since the great siege of Troy, where men also wondered on an horse, was there such a wondering as then. But finally the king asketh this knight concerning the power and virtue of this courser, and prayed him tell the manner of governing him. Anon the horse began to trip and dance, when this knight laid hand on his rein and said: "Sir, there is no more to say than when ye list to ride anywhere ye must twirl in his ear a pin, of which I shall tell you betwixt us two. Ye must also tell him by name to what place or country ye list to ride. And when ye come where ye list to alight, bid him descend and twirl another pin, for therein lieth the secret of all the contrivance, and he will descend down and do your will, and in that place he will abide; though all the world had sworn the contrary, he shall not be drawn thence nor carried. Or if ye list to bid him go thence, twirl this pin, and he will straightway vanish out of the sight of all folk, and come again, be it by day or by night, when ye list to call him again in such wise as I shall say to you full soon betwixt you and me. Ride when ye list, there is no more to be done."

When this noble doughty king was instructed of that knight and hath conceived justly in his wit the manner and the form of all this contrivance, thus glad and blithe he repaireth to his revelry as before. The bridle is borne unto the tower and kept among his precious jewels. The horse vanished out of their sight, I wot not how; ye get no more of me. And thus in merriment and joy I leave this Cambinskan at feasting with his lords, till well nigh the day began to spring.

Here endeth the first part.
Here followeth the second part.

The nurse of digestion, Sleep, gan wink upon them, and bade them take thought that much drink and labour will have rest, and with yawning mouth he kissed them all, and said it was time to lie down, for blood was in supremacy. "Cherish blood, nature's friend," quoth he. By twos and threes, they thank him yawning, and every wight gan draw to his rest, as sleep bade them, and as seemed to them good. I shall not tell of their dreams; full were their heads of fumosity, which causeth dreaming, but of that no matter. The more part of them slept till fully prime, unless it were Canacee. She was temperate as be most women. For she had liberty of her father to go to rest soon after it was eve. She list not to grow pale nor to appear unfestive on the morrow, and slept her first sleep and then awoke. For she took such a joy in her heart both of her wondrous ring and her mirror that twenty times she changed hue, and in her sleep, for the very remembrance of her mirror, she had a vision. Wherefore, ere the sun gan glide upward, she called on her mistress, who slept hard by, and said that she list to rise. These old women will aye be prudent; wherefore her mistress answered her anon and said: "Madame, whither will ye go thus early? for all the folk be abed." "I will arise," quoth she, "for I list no longer to sleep; and walk about."

Her mistress calleth a great troop of women, and up they rise, full ten or twelve; and up riseth fresh Canacee as ruddy and bright as the young sun that is voyaged four degrees in the Ram. No higher was he when she was ready, and forth she walketh quietly in light array, for the sweet lusty season, to walk and take her pastime with but five or six of her train. And forth in the park she goeth in an alley. The vapour that streamed upward from the earth made the sun to seem ruddy and broad; but natheless it was so fair a sight that it made all their hearts to leap up, what with the season and the morning-time and the birds that she heard sing, for right anon by their song she wist what they meant, and knew all their thought.

If the knot for which every tale is recounted be delayed till the pleasure of them be cold that have hearkened for it long, the savour passeth away more and more for fulsomeness of the prolixity, and for the same reason, methinketh, I should come to the knot and make soon an end of their walking.

Full high amid a withered tree as white as chalk, while Canacee roamed in her pastime, there sat a falcon over her head that with piteous voice so gan to cry that of her wail all the wood resounded. So piteously hath she beaten herself with both her wings that the red blood ran all adown the tree whereon she rested. And ever alike she cried and screamed, and so stabbed herself with her beak, that there is no tiger, nor cruel beast that dwelleth in woods, that would not have wept, if he could weep, for pity of her—so loud she screamed alway. For there was never yet a man alive—if I could describe this falcon well—that heard of such another for fairness both of plumage and nobility of shape, and of all things that may be reckoned. A falcon peregrine she seemed, from a foreign land, and evermore again and again she swooneth for lack of blood, till she is well nigh fallen from the tree.

This fair king's-daughter, that wore on her finger the wondrous ring, through which she understood fully all that any bird may say in his jargon, and could in his jargon answer him again, this Canacee hath understood what this falcon said and well nigh she died for ruth. And to the tree she goeth in haste and looketh pitifully on this falcon, and held wide her kirtle, for well she wist the falcon must fall from the bough, when next it swooned for lack of blood. A long time she stood to watch it, till at the last she spake in such fashion to the hawk as ye shall hear.

"What is the cause, if it may be told, that ye be in this

furious pain of hell? Is this for sorrow of some death or for loss of love? For as I ween these be two causes that bring woe to a gentle heart. It needeth not speak of other harm; for I see you tormenting yourself, which well proveth that either love or fear must occasion your cruel deed, sith I see not that ye are chased by any creature. For love of God, show yourself some mercy, or what may advantage you? for never ere now saw I in this world beast or bird that fared with himself so piteously. In sooth, ye slay me with your sorrow, I have such pity for you. For God's love, come down from the tree and, as I am a true king's-daughter, if I might know the cause verily of your grief, if it lay in my power, I would amend it before night, so help me the great God of nature! And I shall find herbs a-plenty wherewith quickly to heal your hurts."

Then this falcon screamed more piteously than ever, and straightway fell to the ground and lay swooning as dead and like a stone, till Canacee hath taken her in her lap, to await such time as she should awake from her swoon. And after she gan start out of this swoon, she said thus in her hawk's language:

"That pity runneth soon into a gentle heart, that feeleth his fellow-being in pain, is every day proved, as men may behold, both by acts and by book-authority; for gentle heart sheweth gentle deeds. I see well, my fair Canacee, that ye have compassion of my distress, because of the true, womanly benignity that nature hath set in you. Yet not from the hope of faring the better, but to obey your noble heart, and to make others beware by me as the lion is affrighted by beating a dog, even for that cause—while I have leisure and a space to do it—will I confess my woe, ere I pass on." And ever while the one told her sorrow, the other wept as if she would turn to water, till the falcon bade her to be still, and with a sigh thus she said her say:

"Where I was bred (alas! wretched time!) and fostered in a rock of grey marble so tenderly that nothing ailed me, I knew not what adversity was till I could soar far aloft under the sky. Then dwelt a tercelet hard by me that seemed the well of all gentleness. Although he was full of treason and falsehood, it was wrapped in such manner under humble looks, show of truth, courtesy and busy tokens of regard, that no wight would have weened that he could dissemble, so deep in grain he dyed his colours. Even as a serpent hideth him under blossoms till he may see his time to sting, even so doth this god of love, this hypocrite, perform his ceremonies and dutiful attentions and in semblance doth all the observances that accord unto love's gentleness. As in a tomb all the fairness is outward and underneath is the corpse in such guise as ye know, even such was this hypocrite, both cold and hot, and in this wise he served his purpose, so that (save the fiend) none knew what was his mind; till he had wept and lamented so long, and so many a year feigned his service to me, that my heart—too pitiful and too foolish—all innocent of his sovereign malice, and fearful as methought of his death, upon his oath and pledge, granted him love upon this condition, that evermore mine honor and fame should be spared, both privily and openly; that is to say, I gave him, after his deserving, all my heart and all my thought— God knoweth, and he, that I would not on other terms—and took his heart for aye in exchange for mine. But the sooth was said this many a day ago, 'A true wight and a thief think not alike.' And when he saw the thing gone so far that I had granted him my love fully in such wise as I have said, and given him my true heart, as utterly as he swore that he gave me his, straightway this tiger, full of doubleness, fell on his knees, with humility so devout, with reverence so high and, in his look, so like in manner unto a gentle lover, so ravished as it seemed with bliss, that never Jason nor Paris of Troy—Jason? nay certes, nor any other man since Lameth, that was the first of all to love two, as folk wrote of yore, nor ever since the first man was born, could anyone, by a twenty-thousandth part, imitate the sophisms of his cunning, nor be worthy to unbuckle his shoe where it concerneth feigning or doubleness, nor could so thank a person as he did me. It were an heaven to any woman—be she never so knowing—to behold his manner, he so painted and combed at point-device his words as well as his countenance. And I so loved him for his devotedness and for the truth I deemed in his heart, that if it chanced anything grieved him, were it never so little, an I knew of it, methought I felt death wring my heart. And in brief, so far is this thing gone, that my will was his will's instrument; that is to say, my will obeyed his in everything as far as was in reason, keeping the bounds ever of my worship, nor was ever thing so lief and dear to me as he, God wot! nor shall be evermore.

"Longer than a year or two this lasteth that I supposed naught but good of him; but finally it befell that fortune would have him depart out of that place wherein I was. Whether I were woful there is no question; I can describe it not. But one thing I dare tell boldly: I know thereby what is the pain of death, such woe did I feel that he might not tarry. On a day he took his leave of me, so sorrowfully eke that I weened in truth he felt as much woe as I, when I heard him speak and saw his pallor. But I thought natheless he was true, and, to say sooth, that he would come again within a little while, and eke reason would that he must go for his honour, as oft it happeth, so that I made virtue of necessity, and took it well, sith it must be so. As I best might I hid my sorrow from him—Saint John be my witness!—and took him by the hand, and said to him thus: 'Lo! I am all yours; be such as I have been to you, and shall ever be.' It needeth not repeat what he answered. Who can say better than he? Who can do worse? When he hath said all things well, then he hath done. I have heard it said: 'He that shall eat with a fiend needeth a full long spoon therefor.' So at last he must fare on his way, and forth he flyeth till he came where he list. When he thought best to abide, I trow he had in remembrance the text that 'all things, repairing to their kind, rejoice.' Thus men say, methinketh. Men of their own proper nature love newfangledness, as do birds that men feed in cages. For though thou care for them night and day, and strew their cage fair and soft as down, and give them sugar and milk, bread and honey, yet right so soon as the door is raised, they will spurn down their cup with their feet and away to the wood and eat worms. So newfangled be they of diet, and of very nature love novelties, that no gentleness of blood may bind them. So alas the day! fared this tercelet. Though he was gentle-born, fresh and blithe, and goodly for to see, and humble and generous, yet on a time he saw a kite flying, and suddenly he so loved this kite that all his love is clean gone from me, and in this manner he hath broken his troth. Thus the kite hath my love in her service, and I am lorn without remedy."

With that word this falcon gan wail and swooned again in Canacee's bosom.

Great was the lament for the falcon's harm that Canacee made and all her women. They wist not how they might gladden her. But Canacee beareth her home in her kirtle and softly gan wrap her in plasters where with her beak she had hurt herself. Now Canacee can do naught but dig roots out of the ground, to heal this hawk, and make new salves of herbs, precious and fine of hue; from dawn till dark she busieth herself with all her might. And by her bed's head she made a mew and covered it with blue velvets, in sign of the truth that is in women. And without, all the mew is painted green, and there were painted these false fowls such as be all these titlarks, tercelets and owls; and pies, to scream and chide them, were painted eke there for despite.

Thus leave I Canacee with her hawk; no more now will I speak of her ring till the time come again to say how this falcon got her love once more repentant, as the story telleth, by mediation of Cambalus, the king's son of whom I told you. But henceforth I will guide my tale to speak of such battles and adventures that never yet were heard so great wonders.

First I will tell you of Cambinskan, that in his time won many a city; and afterward I will speak of Algarsyf, how he won Theodora for his bride, for whom he was in great peril full oft, had he not been helped by the steed of brass; and afterward I will speak of Cambalo, that fought with the two brethren in the lists for Canacee, ere he might win her. And where I left I will return again.

Part III

Apollo whirleth up his chariot so far aloft that the house of the sly god Mercurius——

(Unfinished.)

The Words of the Franklin

Here follow the words of the Franklin to the Squire, and the words of the Host to the Franklin.

"IN faith, Squire, thou hast quit thee well and frankly I praise full high thy discretion," quoth the Franklin. "Considering thy youth, sir, I applaud thee. Thou speakest so feelingly that, to my thinking, there is none of us that shall be thy peer in eloquence, if thou live; God give thee good fortune and send thee continuance in virtue, for I have great delight of thy speech. I have a son and, by the Trinity, I had liefer than twenty pound worth of land, though right now it were fallen to my lot, that he were a man of such understanding as ye. Fie on possession, unless withal a man be virtuous. I have chid my son, and yet shall, for he list not hearken to virtue; but to play at dice is his wont and to spend and lose all that he hath, and he had liefer talk with a page than commune with any gentle wight where he might have true gentle breeding."

"Straw for your gentle breeding!" quoth our host. "What, Franklin? pardee, sir, well thou wottest that each of you must tell at least a tale or two, or else break his word."

"Sir," quoth the Franklin, "that know I well. I pray you have me not in disdain though I speak to this man a word or two."

"Tell on thy tale without more words."

"Gladly," quoth he, "sir host, I submit unto your will; now hark what I say. I will not withstand you in any way as far as my wits will suffice me. I pray God it may please you, then wot I well it is good enough."

The Franklin's Prologue

The Prologue of the Franklin's Tale.

THESE gentle Bretons in the old time made lays of diverse adventures, rhymed in their early Breton tongue; which lays they sang to their instruments, or else read them for their delight; and one of them I have in remembrance which I shall relate with good-will as best I am able. But, sirs, sith I am a homespun man, I pray you at my beginning to excuse me for my rude speech. Sure I learned never rhetoric; what I speak must be bare and plain; I slept never on the mount of Parnassus, nor learned Marcus Tullius Cicero. Colours I know none, in sooth, but such colours as grow in the mead, or else such as men dye or paint. Colours of rhetoric be too dainty for me; my spirit discerneth naught of such matter. But if ye list ye shall hear my tale.

The Franklin's Tale

Here beginneth the Franklin's Tale.

IN Armorik, that is called Brittany, there was a knight that loved a lady, and did his best diligence to serve her; and many a labour and great emprise he wrought for her, ere she was won. For she was one of the fairest under the heaven, and thereto come of such high kin, that scarce durst this knight, for dread, tell her his woe, his pain and his dolor. But at last, for his worthiness, and especially for his meek obedience, she hath caught such a pity of his suffering, that privily she agreed to take him for her husband and lord, of such lordship, that is, as men have over their wives; and the better to pass their days in bliss, he swore unto her of his free will, as a knight, that never in all his life would he take upon him the mastership against her will, nor cause her jealousy, but obey her, and follow her will in all things, as every lover should do unto his lady; save that he would keep the name of sovereignty, for the sake of his title of husband and knight.

She thanked him and full humbly she said, "Sir, sith of your gentleness ye proffer me so free a rein, I pray to God that there be never, by fault of mine, either war or dissension betwixt us. Sir, I will be your humble, true wife, have here my troth, till my heart cease to beat." Thus be they both in quiet and rest.

For one thing, sirs, I dare safely aver, that friends must obey each other if they will hold company long. Love will not be constrained by mastery. When mastery cometh, the god of love beateth straightway his wings, and farewell! he is gone. Love is a thing free as any spirit. Women by nature desire freedom, and not to be constrained as thralls; and so do men, if I shall say sooth. Lo! he that is most patient in love hath advantage over all. Certainly patience is a high virtue, for, as these clerks say, it compasseth things that rigour shall never compass. Folk should not chide or complain at every mere word. Learn to suffer or else, by my faith, ye shall learn it whether ye will or no. For in this world, sooth, there is no wight that doth not or saith not sometime amiss. A man's ire, sickness, constellation, wine, woe, or changing of humours, causeth him full oft to do, or speak, amiss. A man may not avenge every wrong. According to the occasion, temperance must be shown by every wight, that knoweth to govern himself. And therefore hath this wise worthy knight, in order to live in ease, promised forbearance unto his wife, and full wisely she swore to him that never should there be blame in her.

Here may men witness an humble, wise harmony; thus hath she taken at once her servant and her lord: servant in love, and lord in marriage; therefore he was both in lordship and service. Service? nay, but such service as is higher than lordship, sith he hath both his lady and his love; his lady, certes, and eke his wife, with whom the law of love accordeth. And when he was thus prosperous, he goeth home with his wife to his own country, not far from Penmarch, where was his dwelling, and there he liveth in bliss and in joy.

Who can tell, save him that hath been wedded, the joy, ease and prosperity that is betwixt husband and wife? A year and more this blissful time lasted till the knight, of whom I speak, who was called Arveragus of Kayrrud, made him ready to go and dwell a year or two in England, that was called eke Britain, to seek glory and honour in arms; for he set all his joy in such achievements; and there, the book saith, he dwelled two years.

Now I will stint of this Arveragus and speak of his wife Dorigen, that loveth her husband as her soul. For his absence she sigheth and weepeth, as these noble wives do, when it liketh them. She mourneth, complaineth, waketh, waileth, fasteth; desire for his presence so distresseth her, that all this wide world she setteth at naught. Her friends, that knew her heavy heart, comfort her in all that they can; they preach unto her, night and day they tell her that without cause, alas! she slayeth herself, and with all their diligence they show unto her every kind attention possible in such a case, to make her leave her heaviness.

By degrees, as ye all know, men may engrave in a stone so long that some figure will be imprinted therein. So long have they comforted her that, by hope and argument, she hath received the imprint of her consolation, through which her great sorrow gan assuage; she could not alway endure in such frenzy. And eke, in all this grief, Arveragus hath sent letters home unto her of his welfare, and that he would return hastily; else had this sorrow slain her heart. Her friends saw that her sorrow gan lessen, and prayed her, upon their knees, for God's sake to come and roam in company, to drive her dark fantasy away; and finally she consented, for she saw well that it was for the best.

Now her castle stood fast by the sea, and often she walked with her friends to disport her upon the lofty bank, whence she saw many a ship and barge sailing their course whither they list to sail; but then was that parcel of her woe. For full oft to herself she saith, "Alas! is there no ship, of so many as I see, will bring home my lord? Then were my heart all cured of its bitter stinging pain."

At another time she would sit there pensive, and cast her eyes downward from the brink. But when she saw the grisly, dark rocks, her heart would so quake for very fear, that she might not support herself upon her feet. Then would she sit down upon the green, and piteously gaze out on the sea, and with forlorn and sorrowful sighs, say thus: "Eternal God, that leadest the world through thy providence by a sure control, nothing dost thou perform, as men say, in vain; but, Lord, these grisly, fiendly, black rocks, that seem rather a foul confusion of work than the fair creation of such a perfectly wise and steadfast God, why have ye wrought this unreasonable work? For to my wit, neither east, west, north, nor south, is there man, beast or bird to whom it doth good, but rather harm. See ye not, Lord, how it destroyeth mankind? Although they be not in remembrance, rocks have slain an hundred thousand of mankind, which is so fair a part of thy work, that thou madest it like to thine own image. Then seemed it ye had a great fondness for mankind; but how then may it be that to destroy it ye make such means as do no good, but ever harm? I wot well that by arguments, as it pleaseth them, clerks will say all is for the best, though I cannot discern the causes. But may that God which made the wind to blow preserve my lord! this is mine only prayer. I leave to clerks all disputation; but would to God that all these dark rocks were sunk into hell for his sake! These rocks slay mine heart for fear." This would she say, full piteously weeping.

Her friends saw that it was no alleviation, but grief for her, to roam by the sea, and planned to disport themselves somewhere else. They led her by rivers and springs and eke in other delectable places; they danced and they played at tables and chess.

So on a day, in the morning, they go unto a garden nearby in which they had made their preparation of victuals and of other diversions, and took their pleasure all day long. And this was on the sixth morn of May, that, with his soft showers, had painted this garden full of blossoms and of leaves; and the craft of man's hand had arrayed it so curiously that never, in sooth, was there garden of such glory, unless it were paradise itself. The odour and the fresh sight of flowers would have made any heart for to leap that ever was born, unless too great sickness, or sorrow, held it in pain; so full of beauty and delight was the place. And after dinner, they gan to dance, and eke sing, save only Dorigen, who made alway her complaint and her moan; for she saw not going on the dance him that was her husband and eke her love. But natheless she must tarry yet a time, and with good hope she let slide her sorrow.

Upon this dance amongst others, there danced before Dorigen a squire, that was fresher, I deem, and gaylier clad than the month of May. He singeth and danceth, surpassing any man that is, or was sith the beginning of the world. Therewith, if one should describe him, he was one of the best-looking men alive; young, strong, virtuous, rich, and wise, well-beloved, and held in great esteem. And briefly, to tell the truth, this lusty squire, Venus' servant, who was called Aurelius, unbeknown at all to this Dorigen, had loved her best of any creature, two years and more, as was his fate, and never durst he tell her his grief; but drank in full measure all his pain. He was in despair; nothing durst he say, save that in his songs he would reveal somewhat his woe, in a general complaining; he said he loved but was beloved not. Of such matter he made many lays, songs, complaints, rondeaux and ballads, of how he durst not speak his sorrow but must needs suffer torments, as doth a fury in hell; and he said he must die, as for Narcissus did Echo, that durst not tell her pain. In no other manner than ye hear me describe durst he betray his woe to her; save that, peradventure, at dances, where young folk observe their ceremonies, it may well be that he looked on her countenance, in such wise as a man that asketh grace; but nothing she wist of his thoughts. Natheless, ere they went thence, because he was her neighbour, and a man of rank and esteem, and she had known him for a long time, it happed that they fell in speech; and more and more Aurelius drew forth unto his purpose, and when he saw his time, he spake.

"Madame," quoth he, "by God that created this world, I would, the day that your Arveragus went over the sea, that I had gone whence never I should have come back; for I wot well my service is in vain. My only guerdon is the breaking of my heart. Madame, take pity upon my woe; for with a word ye may slay or save me. Would to God that I were buried here at your feet. I have no opportunity now to speak more; have mercy, sweet, or ye will slay me!"

She gan look upon Aurelius: "Is this your desire," quoth she, "and say ye so? Never before I wist what ye meant. But now that I know your purpose, Aurelie, never by that God that gave me soul and breath shall I be untrue wife, in word or work, so far as I know thereof; I will be his, to whom I am knit; take this of me as final answer." But after that she said thus in play: "Aurelie," quoth she, "by heaven's king, I would yet grant you to be your love, sith I see you lament so piteously. Lo! on that day that, from end to end of Brittany, ye remove all the rocks, stone by stone, so that they hinder no ship nor boat from passing—I say, when ye have made the coast so clean of rocks that there is not a stone visible, then will I love you best of all men; have here my utmost pledge."

"Is there no other grace in you," quoth Aurelius. "No, by that Lord that made me!" quoth she, "for I wot well it shall never betide. Let such follies pass out of your heart. What delight in living should a man have to go love the wife of another man that hath control over her body?"

Sore sigheth Aurelius full oft. Woe was him, when he heard

this, and with a sorrowful heart he replied thus: "Madame," quoth he, "this were an impossible thing! Then must I die of horrid, sudden death." And with that word straightway he turned him away. Then came many of her other friends, and roamed up and down in the garden-walks, and wist nothing of this event, but began on a sudden new revelry till the bright sun lost his colour, for the horizon had bereft the sun of his beams; this is as much as to say it was night. And home they go in joy and in gladness, save only—alas!—wretched Aurelius. He is gone to his house with sorrowful heart; he seeth he may not escape his death. He seemed to feel his heart grow cold; up to the heaven he gan raise his hands, and down he set him on his bare knees, and said his orison in his raving. For very woe he went out of his wits. He wist not what he spake, but with piteous heart thus maketh he his plaint to the gods, and first unto the sun: "Apollo," he said, "god and governor of every plant, herb, blossom, tree, that givest, according to thy declination, to each of them its time and season, even as thy dwelling changeth low or high, lord Phœbus, cast thy merciful gaze on me, wretched Aurelie, that am quite forsaken. Lo, lord! my lady hath sworn my death without guilt, but let thy goodness have some pity upon my dying heart. For I wot well, if it liketh you, lord Phœbus, that, save my lady, ye may help me the best. Now vouchsafe that I may describe unto you in what I may be helped and in what manner.

"Your blissful sister, Lucina the bright, that is chief goddess and queen of the sea, although Neptunus be king in that realm, yet she is empress above him. Lord, ye know well that as her desire is to be quickened and illumined by your flame, for which she followeth you diligently, even so the sea by nature desireth to follow her, that is goddess in the sea and in rivers great and small. Wherefore, lord Phœbus, perform this miracle, or let mine heart burst; this is my petition: Pray her now, at the next opposition that shall take place when thou art in the sign of the Lion, pray her to bring so great a flood that it shall overtop by five fathoms at the least the highest rock in Armorik Brittany; and let this flood endure two years. Then certes I may cry unto my lady: 'Keep your troth, the rocks be away!' Lord Phœbus, perform for me this miracle; pray her that she go no faster course than ye; I say, pray your sister that she go no faster course than ye during these two years. Then shall she ever be just at full, and spring-flood last both night and day. And unless she vouchsafe in such wise to grant me my sovereign lady dear, pray her to sink every rock into her own dark region under ground, wherein Pluto dwelleth; else nevermore shall I win my lady. Unto thy temple in Delphos will I go barefoot; lord Phœbus, see the tears on my cheek, and have some compassion of my pain." And with that word he fell down swooning, and long time he lay in a trance. His brother, that knew of his suffering, caught him up and brought him to bed. Thus desperate in grief and torment, I leave this woful creature lying. Let him choose, for all I reck, whether he will live or perish.

Arveragus, with prosperity and great glory, as he that is the flower of chivalry, is come home with other worthy folk. Blissful art thou now, O thou Dorigen! that hast in thine arms thy lusty husband, the fresh knight, the worthy man of battle, that loveth thee as his own heart's life. He list not to fancy whether any wight, while he was away, had spoken to her of love; he had no suspicion of it. He thinketh naught of such a thing, but danceth, jousteth and maketh her good cheer; and thus I leave them living in joy and bliss, and of sick Aurelius will I tell.

In languor and frenzied torment lay wretched Aurelius two years and more, ere he might set foot on the earth. Comfort in this time had he none, save of his brother, that was a clerk; he knew of all this woe and trouble; for in sooth to none other creature durst he say a word of this matter. Under his breast he bare it more secret than ever did Pamphilus for Galatea. His breast was whole, to look on without, but aye in his heart was the keen arrow; and well ye know that in surgery the cure of a wound healed only on the surface is perilous, unless men may touch the arrow, or come thereat. His brother wept and wailed privily, till at last he remembered him, that while he was at Orleans, in France—as young clerks, that be eager to read curious arts, seek in every nook and corner to learn particular sciences—he remembered him that on a day at Orleans, he saw a book of natural magic, which his fellow, who was at that time a candidate in law, although he was there to learn another art, had privily left upon his desk; which book spake much of operations, touching the eight and twenty houses that belong to the moon, and such foolishness, as is not worth a fly in our days; for the faith of the holy church, in our belief, suffereth no illusion to distress us. And when he remembered him of this book, his heart gan dance anon for joy, and he said privily to himself: "My brother shall be cured in haste; for I am sure that there be arts, by which men make such diverse appearances as these subtle jugglers contrive in play. For oft I have heard tell that jugglers at feasts have caused water to come into a great hall and a barge to row up and down therein. Sometimes there hath seemed to come a grim lion, and sometimes flowers to spring as in a meadow; sometimes a vine, with red and white grapes; sometimes a castle, built all of stone and lime; and when it hath pleased them, straightway they voided it. Thus it seemed to the sight of every man.

"Now then I conclude thus, that if I could find some old comrade at Orleans, that hath these mansions of the moon in remembrance, or other natural magic of the heavens, he should certainly cause my brother to have his love. For with an appearance a clerk may make it seem to a man's sight that the black rocks of Brittany be voided, each and all, and that ships come and go by the brink, and cause this to endure in such form a day or two; thus were my brother cured of his woe. Then Dorigen must needs keep her pledge, or at least he shall put her to shame."

Why should I make longer tale of this? He came unto his brother's bed, and such comforting reasons he gave him for going to Orleans, that straightway up he started and forth then on his way he is gone, in hope to be relieved of his care.

When they were come almost to that city, within two or three furlongs, they met a young clerk roaming by himself, who greeted them discreetly in Latin, and after that he spake what was wondrous. "I know," quoth he, "the cause of your coming;" and ere they went a foot further, he told them all that was in their thoughts. This clerk of Brittany asked him of the fellows whom he had known in the old days; and he answered him that they were dead, for which he wept full many a tear. Aurelius lighted down from his horse, and went home with this magician to his house, and made him full content. He lacked no meat or drink that might please him; so well equipped a house Aurelius saw never in his life before. Ere they went to supper he showed him forests and parks full of wild deer; there he saw harts with their high horns, the greatest that ever were seen. He saw an hundred of them slain with hounds, and some bleeding bitterly with arrows. When these wild deer were voided, upon a fair river he saw falconers that had killed a heron with their hawks. Then he saw knights jousting in a plain; and after this, he did him such pleasure as to show him his lady in a dance, on which, as it seemed, he himself danced. And when this master, that wrought this magic, saw it was time, he clapped his two hands, and farewell! our revelry was all gone. And yet they had never removed from the house while they saw all these wonderful sights, but they sat still all three in his study, where his books were, none other wight with them. This master called his squire to him and said thus: "Is our supper ready? It is almost an hour, I warrant, since I bade you to prepare it, and these worthy men went with me into my study, where my books be kept."

"Sir, when it liketh you," quoth this squire, "it is all ready, though ye wish it right now."

"It is best, then, that we go sup," quoth he, "these amorous folk sometimes must have refreshment." After supper, they fell into discussion what should be this master's guerdon for removing all the rocks of Brittany from the Gironde to the mouth of the Seine. He drove a hard bargain and swore he would not—so God save him!—take less than a thousand pound, nor would he go gladly for that sum.

With blissful heart, Aurelius answered anon thus: "Fie on a thousand pound! I would give this wide world if I were lord of it. This bargain is fully driven, for we be accorded. Ye shall be paid truly, by my faith! but look well now that, by no negligence or sloth, ye delay us here longer than to-morrow."

"Nay, have here my faith as pledge," quoth this clerk.

Aurelius, when he list, went to bed, and rested well nigh all that night. What with his labour and hope of bliss, his woful heart had a lull of its pain. Upon the morrow, when it was light, Aurelius and this magician took the straight way to Brittany, and went down where they would abide; and this, as the books put me in mind, was the cold, frosty season of December.

Phœbus, that in his hot declination had shone as the burnished gold with glittering beams, waxed now old, of a hue like latten; for now he lighted adown in Capricorn, where, I must needs say, he shone full pale. The bitter frosts, with the sleet and rain, had destroyed the green in every close. Janus sitteth by the fire, with double beard, and drinketh the wine from his bugle-horn; before him standeth brawn of the tusked boar, and every lusty man "Nowel" crieth.

Aurelius, in all that ever he is able, maketh cheer and reverence unto his master, and prayeth him either to do his best to bring him out of his wretched pain, or to pierce his heart with a sword. This subtle clerk hath such ruth of him, that night and day he speedeth him to watch for a time for his result; that is to say, to make an illusion, by such an appearance or juggler's trick (I know not terms of astrology), that Dorigen and every wight should ween and confess that the rocks of Brittany were away, or else that they were sunk under ground. So at last he hath hit upon his time to make his wretched mummery of superstitious cursedness. He brought forth his Toletan tables, full well corrected, so that there lacked nothing, neither his round periods nor his separate years, nor his roots, nor his other data, such as be his centres and his arguments, and his fitting proportionals for his exact quantities in every thing; and by the working of his eighth sphere, he knew full well how far Alnath was removed from the head of that fixed Aries which is in the ninth sphere above it; full subtly he calculated all this. When he had found his first mansion, he knew the rest by proportion and knew well the arising of his moon, both in whose face, and in what term of the zodiac, and in every respect; and knew full well the moon's house according to its operation; and knew also his other observances for the causing of such illusions and misfortunes as heathen folk wont to deal with in those days. Wherefore he tarried no longer, but contrived by his magic that, for a week or two, it seemed that all the rocks were away.

Aurelius, who is still despairing whether he shall have his love or fare amiss, awaiteth this miracle night and day, and when he knew that there was no hindrance, and that these rocks were all voided, down he fell anon at his master's feet, and said, "I, woful wretch, thank you, lord, and lady mine Venus, that have helped me out of my desolate cares." And forth he hath held his way to the temple, where he knew he should see his lady, and straightway, when he saw his time, with heart adread and full humble countenance, he hath saluted his dear, sovereign lady: "My true lady," quoth this woful man, "whom I love best and most fear, and whom of all this world I were most loath to displease, were it not that I have for you such a malady, that straightway I must die here at your feet, I would not tell how woe-begone I have been, save that certes I must either die or lament; guiltless, with very pain, ye slay me. But though of my death ye have no pity, yet take counsel, ere ye break your troth.

Repent, for high God's sake, ere ye slay me because I love you. For, madame, ye wot well what ye promised; not that I claim of you anything by right, my sovereign lady, but of your grace. At a certain spot in yonder garden, ye wot well what ye promised me; and ye plighted me your troth in mine hand to love me best, God wot ye said so, although I be unworthy thereof. Madame, I speak it more for your honour than to save even now my heart's life; I have done as ye commanded me; and if ye vouchsafe, ye may go and behold. Do as ye list, have in remembrance your promise, for quick, or dead, right there ye shall find me. In you it lieth wholly to let me die or live; for well I wot the rocks be away!"

He taketh his leave, and she standeth astounded; in all her face there was not a drop of blood. She weened never to have fallen into such a trap. "Alas," quoth she, "that this ever should betide! For I weened never, by any possibility, that such a prodigy or marvel might happen. It is against the process of nature." And home she goeth, a sorrowful wight. Scarce, for very fear, could she walk; all of a day or two she weepeth, waileth and swooneth, that it was ruth to see; but to no wight told she why; for Arveragus was gone out of town. But with face pale and with full sorrowful cheer, she spake to herself, and in her complaint said as ye shall be told.

"Alas!" quoth she, "I cry out against thee, Fortune, that hast bound me unaware in thy chain, to escape which I wot of no release save only death, or else dishonour; one of these two it behooveth me to choose. Natheless I had liefer die, than suffer a shame of my body, or know myself false, or lose my good repute; and in sooth I may be quit of these by my death. Hath there not ere this many a noble wife—hath not many a maid slain herself, rather than do trespass with her body? Yea, certes; lo! these stories bear witness.

"When thirty cursed tyrants had slain Phidon, at a feast in Athens, they commanded his daughters to be seized and brought before them in scorn, naked, to sate their foul desire; and they made them dance in their father's blood on the pavement—may God punish them! For which these woful maidens, in fear, rather than lose their maidenhood, leapt privily into a well, and drowned themselves, as the books say.

"They of Messena eke caused men to seek out fifty maidens of Lacedæmonia, whom they would dishonour; but there was none of that company that was not slain, and chose rather, with a glad will, to die, than consent to be robbed of her maidenhood. Why then should I be in fear to die?

"Lo, eke, Aristoclides, the tyrant, loved a maid named Stymphalides, that on a night, when her father was slain, went straight unto Dian's temple, and seized the image in her two hands, from which she would never depart. No wight could tear away her hands from it, till right in the self-same place she was slain. Now sith those maidens so scorned to be disgraced by man's desire, surely a wife methinketh ought rather to slay herself than be disgraced.

"What shall I say of Hasdrubal's wife, that slew herself at Carthage? For when she saw that the Romans had won the town, she took all her children and leapt into the fire, and chose rather to die than that any Roman should do her dishonour.

"Hath not Lucrece, alas! slain herself at Rome, when she was oppressed of Tarquin, for it seemed to her a shame to live when she had lost her fair repute.

"The seven maidens of Miletus eke have slain themselves,

for mere dread and woe, rather than suffer the folk of Gaul
to oppress them. More, I ween, than a thousand stories could I
tell now touching this matter. When Abradates was slain, his
fond wife slew herself, and let her blood flow into her husband's
wounds, deep and wide, and said, 'At least there shall no wight
disgrace my body, if I may prevent.'

"Why should I tell more ensamples hereof, sith so many have
slain themselves far rather than they would be disgraced? I
will conclude that it is better for me to slay myself, than be
disgraced so. I will be true unto Arveragus, or else slay myself
in some way, as did Demotio's daughter dear, because she would
not be disgraced.

"O Scedasus! it is full great pity, alas! to read how thy
daughters died, that slew themselves for the same reason. As
great a pity, or greater, how the Theban maiden slew herself
for Nicanor, even for the same woful cause. Another Theban
maiden did even so, for one of Macedonia had oppressed her,
and she atoned for her shame by her death. What shall I say
of Niceratus' wife, that slew herself in such a case? How true,
eke, to Alcibiades was his love, that chose rather to die than
suffer his body to be unburied; lo, what a wife was Alcestis!
What saith Homer of good Penelope? All Greece knoweth
how she was chaste. Of Laodomia, pardee, it is written that
when Protesilaus was slain at Troy, she would live no longer
after his day. The same can I tell of noble Portia; without
Brutus, to whom she had yielded her heart all whole, she could
not live. The perfect wifehood of Artemisia is honoured
throughout all heathendom. O Queen Teuta! thy wifely chastity
may be a mirror unto all wives. The same thing I say of Bilia,
Valeria and Rhodogune."

Thus lamented Dorigen for a day or two, purposing ever that she would die. Natheless, upon the third night, home came this worthy man Arveragus, and asked her why she so grievously wept. And she gan weep ever the more. "Alas!" quoth she, "that I was born! Thus have I said, thus have I promised—" and told him as ye have heard before; it needeth not rehearse it to you.

This husband, in friendly wise, answered with glad cheer and said as I shall tell you: "Is there naught else but this, Dorigen?" "Nay, nay," quoth she, "may God help me, verily this is too much, and it were God's will." "Yea, wife," quoth he, "let sleeping dogs lie; peradventure, all may be well yet to-day. Ye shall keep your troth, by my faith! For as God may have mercy on me, I had far liefer be slain, for the true love which I have for you, than ye should not keep and preserve your troth. A man's troth is the highest thing that he can preserve;" and anon with that word he burst out weeping and said, "I forbid you, on pain of death, while life lasteth to you, ever to tell of this mischance to any wight. As best I may, I will endure my woe, nor wear a heavy countenance, lest folk deem, or guess, evil of you." And he called forth a squire and a maid. "Go forth now with Dorigen," quoth he, "and bring her anon to such a place." They take their leave and go on their way; but they wist not why she went thither. He would not tell his purpose to any wight.

Peradventure an heap of you will deem him an ignorant man in this, that he would put his wife in jeopardy; hearken the story ere ye lament for her. She may have better fortune than ye suppose; judge, when ye have heard the tale.

This squire Aurelius, that was so enamoured of Dorigen,

happed by chance to encounter her, amid the town, in the busiest street, as she was prepared to go the straight way toward the garden, where she had made her promise. And he also was going to the garden, for well he espied, when she would go out of her house to any place. Thus, by providence or chance, they met, and he saluted her with glad heart, and asked of her whither she went. And she answered half as she were mad, "Unto the garden as my husband hath bidden me, for to keep my troth, alas! alas!"

Aurelius gan wonder at this, and had in his heart great compassion of her, and of her lamentation, and of Arveragus, the worthy knight that bade her hold unto all she had promised, so loath was he that his wife should break her troth; and in his heart he was seized with great pity of this, so considering the best on every side, that liefer would he abstain from his desire than do so high-churlish and wretched a deed against nobility and all gentleness. Wherefore in few words he said:

"Madame, say to your lord Arveragus that sith I see his great gentleness to you, and eke your grief, that he would liefer have shame (and that were pity), than that ye should break now your troth with me, I would far liefer suffer pain evermore than part the love betwixt you two. I release you, madame, here in your hand, of every bond and security that ye have made to me heretofore, sith the day ye were born. I pledge my troth I shall never reproach you of any promise, and here I take my leave of the truest and the best wife that ever I knew yet in all my days. But let every woman beware of her promise, and take remembrance at last on Dorigen. Thus, without doubt, can a squire do a gentle deed as well as a knight."

She thanketh him, all on her bare knees, and home she is gone unto her husband, and telleth him all, even as ye have heard me say; and be sure, he was so well pleased that it were impossible for me to tell thereof; why should I endite longer of this matter?

Arveragus and Dorigen led forth their life in sovereign bliss. Nevermore was there anger betwixt them; he cherisheth her like a queen; and she was ever true to him. Of these two ye get no more of me.

Aurelius, that hath lost all his pains, curseth the time that he was born. "Alas," quoth he, "alas! that I promised a thousand pound in weight of pure gold unto this philosopher! What shall I do? I see naught but that I am undone. Mine heritage I must needs sell and be a beggar; I may not live here; I should shame all my kindred in this town, unless I might get better grace of this magician. But natheless I will endeavour year by year at certain days to pay him, and thank him for his great courtesy; I will keep my troth; I will not deceive him."

With sad heart he goeth unto his chest and bringeth gold unto this philosopher, to the value, I ween, of five hundred pound, and beseecheth him, of his gentleness, to grant him time to pay the remnant, and said, "Master, I dare make boast that I never failed yet of my troth; for my debt to you shall surely be paid, though it be my lot to go abegging in my bare kirtle. But would ye vouchsafe, upon security, to give me respite of two or three years, then were I fortunate, for else I must sell mine heritage; there is no more to say."

When he had heard these words, this philosopher soberly answered and said, "Have I not kept covenant with thee?" "Yea, certes," quoth he, "well and truly." "Hast thou not had thy lady as pleaseth thee?" "No, no," quoth he, and sorrowfully sigheth. "What was the cause? tell me, if thou canst." Aurelius began anon his tale, and told him as ye have heard before; it needeth not rehearse it unto you.

He said, "Arveragus, of his gentleness, had liefer die in sorrow and woe, than that his wife were false of her troth." He told him also of Dorigen's sorrow, how loath she was to be a wicked wife, and that she had liefer die that day, and that she had sworn her troth, through innocence: "She never before heard tell of illusions; that made me have so great pity of her; and even as freely as he sent her to me, as freely I sent her to him again. This is the sum and substance; there is no more to say."

This philosopher answered, "Dear brother, each of you acted gently. Thou art a squire and he is a knight, but God, in his blessed power, forbid that a clerk may not do a gentle deed as well, surely, as any of you. Sir, I release thee of thy thousand pound as if right now thou hadst crept out of the earth, and never ere now hadst known me. For, sir, I will not take a penny of thee for all my craft, nor aught for my labour; thou hast paid well for my victualing; it is enough, have good day, and farewell!" And he took his horse and went forth.

Lordings, this question now would I ask: Which, as seemeth to you, was the most liberal? Now tell me, ere ye go farther. I can say no more; my tale is at an end.

Here is ended the Franklin's Tale.

The Canon's Yeoman's Prologue

The Prologue of the Canon's Yeoman's Tale.

WHEN the life of Saint Cecilia* was ended, ere we had ridden fully five miles, at Boghton-under-Blee a man gan overtake us that was clad in black clothes, and underneath he had a white surplice. His hackney, that was all dappled gray, sweat so that it was wonderful to behold; it seemed as he had spurred three miles. The horse that his yeoman rode upon eke so sweat that it scarce might go. He was all flecked as a magpie with foam, that stood full thick about the poitrel. A doubled wallet lay on his crupper; it seemed that he carried little raiment. This worthy man rode all light-clad for summer, and I gan wonder in my heart what he was, till I espied how his cloak was sewed to his hood; for which, when I had considered long, I deemed him to be some canon. His hat hung down at his back by a string, for he had ridden more than a walk or trot; he had spurred aye as he were mad. Under his hood he had a burdock leaf against the sweat and to keep his head from the sun. Eh, but it was joy to see him sweat! His forehead dripped as a still, full of plantain and of pellitory. And when he was come, he gan call out, "God save this jolly company! I have pricked fast on your account, because I would overtake you and ride in this merry company." His yeoman eke was full courteous and said, "Sirs, this morn I saw you ride out of your hostelry, and warned my lord and master here, that is full fain to ride with you for his diversion; he loveth dalliance."

---

*The subject of the Second Nun's Tale, which in the complete *Canterbury Tales* immediately precedes this Prologue.

"Friend," then said our host, "God give thee good luck for thy warning, for it would seem, certes, thy lord is wise, and I may well think so. I dare lay my money also he is full jocund. Can he tell us ever a merry tale or two, with which he may gladden this company?"

"Who, sir? My lord? Yea, yea, without doubt; he knoweth enough and to spare of mirth and jollity; trust me, sir, also an ye knew him as well as I do, ye would marvel how craftily and well he can work, and that eke in sundry ways. He hath taken many a great emprise upon him, which would be full hard for any that is here to carry out, unless they learn it of him. As homely as he rideth amongst you, yet if ye knew him, it would be for your advantage; ye would not forego his acquaintance for much wealth, I dare stake all that I possess. He is a man of high discretion; I warn you, he is a passing man."

"Well," quoth our host, "I pray thee then tell me, is he a clerk, or no? Tell what he is."

"Nay, faith, he is greater than a clerk," said this yeoman, "and in few words, host, I will tell you somewhat of his craft. I say, my lord knoweth such subtlety (but ye may not learn from me all his craft and yet I help somewhat in his working) that all this ground on which we be riding till we come to Canterbury-town he could turn clean inside-out and pave it all of silver and gold."

And when this yeoman had thus spoken unto our host, he said, *"Ben'cite!* this thing to me is a wondrous marvel, sith thy lord is of so high discretion because of which men should reverence him, that he recketh so little of his worship. In truth I vow his cloak is not worth a mite; it is all dirty and torn also. Why is thy lord so sluttish, I pray thee, and yet hath power to

211

buy better clothes, if his deed accord with thy tale of him? Tell me that; and that I beseech thee."

"Why?" quoth this yeoman, "wherefore ask me? So help me God, he shall never prosper. (But I will not avow what I say and therefore, I beseech you, keep it secret.) I believe in faith, he is too wise. That which is overdone will not come out aright; as clerks say, it is a vice. Wherefore in that I hold him blind and foolish. For when a man hath a wit over-great, full oft it happeth him to misuse it. So doth my lord, and that grieveth me much. God amend it; I can say no more to you."

"No matter of that, good yeoman," our host said, "sith thou wotst of the cunning of thy lord, I pray thee heartily tell what he doth, sith he is so sly and crafty. Where dwell ye, if it may be told?"

"In the suburbs of a town," quoth he, "lurking in corners and blind lanes, where robbers and thieves hold by nature their secret fearful dwelling, as they that dare not show their presence; even so we fare, if I shall say sooth to thee."

"Now let me talk to thee yet," quoth our host; "wherefore art thou so discoloured of thy face?"

"Peter!" quoth he, "God give it sorrow, I am so used to blow in the fire, that I ween it hath changed my colour. I am not wont to peer into any mirror, but to toil sore and learn to multiply. We become mazed and pore ever into the fire, yet for all that we fail of our hopes for we lack ever our result. We delude many folk and borrow gold, be it a pound, or two, or ten, or twelve, or many sums larger, and make them ween at the least that of one pound we can make two. Yet it is false, but we have aye faith that we may do it, and we grope after it. But that knowledge is so far beyond us, we may not overtake it, though we had sworn to, it glideth away so quickly; it will make us beggars at last."

While this yeoman was talking thus, this canon drew near and heard all which this yeoman spake, for he had ever suspicion of men's speech. For Cato saith that he that is guilty deemeth verily that all things be spoken of him. That was the cause why he drew him so near to his yeoman, to hearken all his speech; and thus he said then unto his yeoman, "Hold thy peace and speak no more words, for if thou do, thou shalt pay for it dear; thou slanderest me in this company, and makest known eke what thou shouldst hide."

"Yea," quoth our host, "tell on, whatsoever befall; reck not a mite for all his threatening."

"In faith, no more I do but little," quoth he.

And when this canon saw that it would be no else than this yeoman would tell his privacy, he fled away, for very shame and sorrow.

"Aye," quoth the yeoman, "here shall be sport; all now that I know will I tell anon. Sith he is gone, the foul fiend kill him! For never hereafter, I promise you, will I meet with him, for penny nor for pound. He that first brought me into that sport, may he have sorrow and shame ere he die! For, by my fay, it hath been bitter earnest to me; I feel that well, whatsoever any man saith. And yet for all my pain and grief, for all my sorrow and labour and misfortune, I could in no wise ever leave it. Now would to God my wit might be sufficient to tell all that pertaineth to that craft! Natheless I will tell you part; sith my lord is gone, I will not spare him; such things as I know I will speak."

Here endeth the Prologue of the Canon's Yeoman's Tale.

The Canon's Yeoman's Tale

Here beginneth the Canon's Yeoman his Tale.

SEVEN years have I dwelt with this canon and never the better am I for his science. Thereby have I lost all that I had and, God wot, so have many more than I. Where I was wont to be right gay of clothing and of other fine gear, now I may wear a stocking on mine head; and where my colour was both fresh and ruddy, now is it wan and leaden of hue. Whosoever practiseth this art shall have sorrow therefor. Mine eyes are still bleared of my toil. Lo, what advantage it is to multiply! That slippery science hath made me so bare that I have naught left wheresoever I go. And thereby am I so deep in debt for gold that I have borrowed, that truly while I live I shall never repay it. Let every man forevermore beware by me! Whatsoever man turneth him thereto, I hold his thrift shall be at an end if he continue. So help me God, he shall gain naught thereby, but empty his purse and make thin his wits; and when, by his madness and folly, he hath staked and lost his own goods, then thereto he exciteth other folk to lose their goods even as he himself hath done. For it is joy and content unto rogues to have their fellows in pain and distress. Thus once was I taught of a clerk; but of that no matter; I will speak of our labours.

When we be where we shall practise our elvish craft, we seem wondrous wise, our terms be so clerkly and strange. I blow the fire till mine heart fainteth. Why should I tell all the proportions of the things which we work upon, as on five or six ounces of silver, or perchance some other quantity, and busy me to tell you the names of iron scales, of orpiments and burnt bones, that be ground full fine into powder? And how all is placed in an earthen pot, and salt put in, and also, before these powders that I speak of, paper and many other things, and well covered with a plate of glass? And how the pot and glasses are sealed with clay, that naught of the air may pass out? And of the easy and eke the brisk fire which was made, and of the trouble and the woe that we had in sublimating our substances, and in the amalgaming and the calcining of quicksilver, called crude mercury. For all our sleights, we cannot attain unto our end. Our orpiment and our sublimed mercury, our litharge eke ground on a porphyry slab—to use of these a certain number of ounces of each helpeth us naught; our labour is in vain. Nor may the vapourizing of our spirits, nor eke the substances that remain thereafter, avail us aught in our working; for lost is all our labour and toil, and lost also, in twenty devil ways, is all the money which we stake upon it.

There be eke full many other things that pertain unto our craft; though I cannot rehearse them in their order, because I am a skilless wight, yet will I tell them as I call them to mind, though I cannot set each in its class: as Armenian clay, borax, verdigris, sundry vessels made of glass and earth, our pots, our descensories, vials, sublimating vessels, crucibles, gourds, alembics and other such vessels, dear enough at a leek's worth. It needeth not to rehearse every one: reddening waters, bull's gall, arsenic, sal ammoniac, and brimstone; and eke many an herb could I tell, as agrimony, valerian, lunary, and other such if I list to take the time. Our lamps are burning both day and night to bring about our end, if may be.

We have eke our furnaces for calcination and for the albification of water, our unslaked lime, chalk, white of egg, diverse powders, dung, ashes, clay, waxed bags, vitriol, saltpeter, and divers sorts of fire made of wood and charcoal, salt of tartar, alkali, prepared salt, calcined and coagulated substances, clay made with horse-hair or man's-hair, oil of tartar, alum, glass, yeast, herbs, crude tartar, red orpiment, our substances for absorbing and drinking-in others; our citronizing of silver; our cementing and fermentation; our moulds, assaying-vessels and many things more.

I will tell you, as was also taught me, the four spirits and the seven bodies in their order, as oft I have heard my lord name them. The first spirit is called quicksilver, the second orpiment, the third sal ammoniac and the fourth brimstone. The seven bodies, lo! here are they eke: Sol is gold, Luna we call silver, Mars iron, Mercury we name quicksilver, Saturn lead, Jupiter tin and Venus copper, by the souls of my forefathers!

Whosoever will practise this cursed craft shall alway be poor; for all the goods he spendeth thereon he shall lose, I have no doubt. Whoso that list to display his folly, let him come forth and learn multiplying. And every man that hath aught in his purse, let him appear and wax a philosopher. Perchance because that craft is so light to learn? Nay, nay, God wot, be he friar or monk, priest or canon, or any other man, though he sit at his book day and night learning this foolish elvish lore, all is in vain and, pardee, much worse! To teach this subtlety to an ignorant man, fy! speak not thereof; it may not be. Knoweth he book-lore, or knoweth he none, in the end he shall find it all the same. For, by my salvation, both the two end alike well in multiplying, when they have done all they may; that is to say, they fail both the two.

THE CANON'S YEOMAN'S TALE

Yet I forgot to make rehearsal of corrosive waters, of metal filings, of mollification of bodies, and eke of their induration; oils, ablutions and fusible metal; to tell all would outdo any great volume in the world; wherefore, as seemeth best, I will stint now of all these names; for I trow I have told you enough to raise a fiend, look he never so fierce.

Ah, nay! let be! we seek eagerly each and all for the philosopher's stone, called Elixir; for if we had him then were we secure enough; but I make mine avow unto God in heaven, for all our craft and sleight, when we have done our all, he will not come to us. He hath made us spend mickle goods, for sorrow of which we wax almost mad, but that hope creepeth into our hearts, making us suppose ever, though we be in sore trouble, that we shall be relieved by him afterward. Such supposing and hope are sharp and cruel; I warn you well, it is ever to seek, and that future tense hath made men, by trusting thereto, part from all that ever they had; yet of that craft they cannot wax weary, for it is a bitter sweetness unto them, so it seemeth; for had they naught but a sheet to wrap them in at night and a clout to walk in by day, yet would they sell them and spend all on this art; they cannot stint till nothing be left. And evermore, wheresoever they go, men may know them by the smell of brimstone. They stink for all the world like a goat. Their savour is so hot and rammish that, though a man be a mile from them, the savour shall infect him, trust me. Lo! thus, by smell and threadbare garb, men may know these folk, if they list. And if a man will privily ask them why they be clothed so unthriftily, right anon they will whisper in his ear and say, that if they were espied, men would slay them because of their science. Lo! thus doth this folk betray the innocent!

Pass over this; I turn to my tale. Ere the pot be set on the fire with a certain quantity of metals, my lord, and no man save him, tempereth them—now he is gone, I dare speak boldly—for, as men say, he knoweth his craft well; yet, though I wot well he hath such a reputation, full oft he runneth into a fault. And wit ye how? full oft it so happeth that the pot breaketh in pieces, and farewell! all is gone! These metals be of so great a violence that our walls may not resist them unless they be wrought of lime and stone. They pierce through the walls and some of them sink into the earth (thus at times have we lost many a pound), some are scattered all about the floor and some leap into the roof. I trow there is no doubt, though the fiend showeth him not in our sight, that he be with us, the very rogue himself! for in hell, where he is lord and master, there is not more woe nor rancour nor ire. When our pot is broke, as I have said, every man chideth and holdeth him ill used. One saith, it was along of the way the fire was made; another saith nay, it was the blowing (then was I afeard, for that was mine office); "Straw!" quoth the third, "ye be stupid and foolish; it was not tempered as it ought to have been." "Nay, stint!" quoth the fourth, "and hearken to me; our fire was not made of beech-wood, that is the cause and no other I swear." I cannot tell what it was along of, but I wot well great strife was amongst us.

"What! there is no more to do," quoth my lord, "I will beware hereafter of these perils; I am right sure that the pot was cracked. Be that as it may, be not ye confounded; let the floor be swept at once, as usual; pluck up your hearts and be glad and blithe."

The muck was swept on an heap, and a canvas was cast

on the floor and all this muck thrown into a sieve and sifted and picked over and over.

"Pardee!" quoth one, "there is somewhat of our metal here yet, though we have not all. Though this thing have mischanced now, another time it may turn out well enough; we must needs put our goods in jeopardy. A merchant, pardee! trust me well, may not abide aye in his prosperity; sometimes his goods be drowned in the ocean, and sometimes cometh it safe to land."

"Peace," quoth my lord, "the next time I will take care that our experiment shall come out quite in another fashion; and unless I do, let me have the blame, sirs; there was some defect in something, I know well."

Another said that the fire was over-hot; but, be it hot or cold, I dare assert that evermore we conclude amiss. We fail of what we desire, and in our madness we rave evermore. And when we be all together, every man seemeth a Solomon; but, as I have heard tell, "all thing which that shineth as the gold is not gold," nor is every apple good that is fair to the eye, howsoever men prate. Right so, lo! fareth it amongst us; he that seemeth the wisest, by Jesu! is most a fool, when it cometh to the proof; and he is a thief, that seemeth truest. That ye shall know, ere I depart from you, what time I have made an end of my tale.

Part II

There is a canon of religion amongst us, who would infect a whole town, though it were as great as Nineve, Rome, Alexandria, Troy and three more such. No man, I ween, though he might live a thousand years, could write down his tricks and his infinite falseness. There is not his peer for falsehood in all this world; for he would so wind him in his strange terms, and speak his words in so sly a fashion, when he would commune with any wight, that, unless he were a fiend like himself, he would make him straightway to dote. Many a man ere this hath he beguiled, and yet shall if he live; and yet men ride and walk many a mile to seek him and have his acquaintance, knowing naught of his false behaviour; and if ye list to hear me, I will tell it all here in your presence.

But ye worshipful religious canons, deem not that I slander your house, although my tale be of a canon. Some rogue, pardee, is in every order, and God forbid that a whole company should rue the folly of one man. To slander you is no wise my purpose, but to correct what is amiss. This tale was told not only for you, but eke for others beside. Ye wot well how, among Christ's twelve apostles, there was no traitor but Judas; then why should all the remnant have censure that were guiltless? For you I say the same; save only this, if ye will hearken my warning: if any Judas be in your convent, remove him betimes, if ye dread at all shame or loss. And be not displeased, I pray you, but hearken what I shall say of this canon.

There was in London a priest, an annualer, that had dwelt there many a year, and was so pleasant and attentive unto the dame, where he was at board, that she would suffer him to pay nothing for food nor clothing, though he lived never so gaily; and spending-silver eke had he enough. Thereof no matter; I will proceed now and tell forth my tale of the canon, that brought confusion upon this priest.

This false canon came on a day unto this priest's chamber, beseeching him to lend him a certain sum of gold, and he would pay it to him again. "Lend me a mark but three days," quoth he, "and I will pay thee on the day. And if so be thou find me false, another day have me hanged by the neck!"

This priest gave him a mark right soon, and this canon thanked him many times, and took his leave and went forth his way, and on the third day brought his money and gave his gold again to the priest, whereof this priest was wondrous glad.

"Certes," quoth he, "it troubleth me not at all to lend a man a noble, or two, or whatsoever sum be in my possession, when he is so true of principle—that he will in no wise break his word; to such a man I can never say nay."

"What! should I be untrue?" quoth this canon. "Nay, that were a new thing to befall. Truth is a thing that I will hold evermore unto that day in which I shall creep into my grave; God forbid else! Believe this as sure as your creed. I thank God, and happy am I to say it, that there was never man yet ill pleased for gold or silver that he lent me, nor ever have I thought falsehood in my heart. And now, sir, sith ye have been so kind to me, and shown me so great gentilesse, I will—somewhat to requite your courtesy—show you of my secrets, and if ye list to learn, I will teach you fully the manner how I can work in philosophy. Take good heed, and ye shall see well with your own eyes that I will do a master-stroke, ere I depart."

"Yea!" quoth the priest, "yea, sir! will ye so? Marie! I pray you heartily." "Truly, sir, at your commandment," quoth the canon, "and else God forbid!"

Lo! how this thief could offer his service! Full sooth is it that such proffered service stinketh, as these old wise folk be witness; and that full soon will I verify by this canon, root of all deceit, that evermore hath delight and gladness in devising how he may bring Christ's people to mischief, such fiendly thoughts are imprinted on his heart. God keep us from his dissimulation!

This priest wist not with whom he dealt, nor was ware of the harm coming unto him. O simple priest! Simple innocent! Anon shalt thou be blinded by thy covetousness. O graceless one! full blind is thy thought, little art thou ware of the deceit which this fox hath contrived for thee! Thou mayst not escape his wily tricks. Wherefore to pass to the end, that bringeth to thy confusion, unhappy man, I will hie me anon to tell thy folly and the falseness eke of that other wretch, as far forth as my skill may allow.

This canon, perchance ye think, was my lord? Sir host, in faith, by the heaven's queen, it was not he, but another canon, that knoweth more subtlety an hundred fold. He hath many a time betrayed folk; it dulleth me to tell of his falsehood. Whenever I speak of it, my cheeks wax red for shame; at least they begin to glow, for of redness I wot right well I have none in my visage; for diverse fumes of metals, which ye have heard me recite, have consumed and wasted my ruddy hue. Now hearken this canon's cursedness!

"Sir," quoth he to the priest, "let your man go for quicksilver, that we may have it anon; and let him bring two or three ounces; and so soon as he cometh, ye shall see a wondrous thing, which ye saw never ere this." "Sir," quoth the priest, "it shall be done." He bade the servant fetch him that thing, and he was already at his call, and went forth and anon came again with the quicksilver, and gave the three ounces to the canon, who laid them down well and fair, and bade the servant bring coals that he might go anon to his work. The coals were straightway fetched and this canon took out of his bosom a crucible and showed it to the priest. "Take this instrument which thou seest," quoth he, "in thy hand, and thyself put therein an ounce of this quicksilver, and begin here, in the name of Christ, to wax a philosopher. There be few to whom I would offer to show thus much of my science. For ye shall see here, by experiment, that anon I will mortify this quicksilver right in your sight, and make it as good silver and pure as there is in your purse, or mine, or elsewhere, and make it malleable; else hold me false and unfit forevermore to be seen amongst folk. I have here a powder, that cost me dear, which shall make good all that I say; for it is the cause of all my cunning which I shall show you. Send your man forth, and let him be without there and shut the door, whilst we be about our privy working, that no man may behold us whilst we work in this philosophy." All was fulfilled in deed as he bade; straightway the servant went out, and his master shut the door, and speedily they went to their labour.

Anon this priest, as the cursed canon bade, set this thing upon the fire, and blew the fire and busied him full intently; and this canon cast a powder into the crucible, I wot not whereof it was made, either of chalk, or of glass, or of somewhat else not worth a fly, to dupe the priest withal; and bade him to pile the coals up high above the crucible; "for in token that I love thee," quoth the canon, "thine own two hands shall perform all things that shall be done here." "Grammercy," quoth the priest, full blithe, and piled the coals as the canon bade. And while he was busy, this fiendly rogue, this false canon—the foul fiend fetch him!—took from his bosom a beechen coal, in which full subtly was made an hollow and therein was put an ounce of silver filings, and the hole was stopped with wax, to keep in the filings.

And understand that this false gin was not made there, but was made before. And I shall tell hereafter of other things which he brought with him; ere he came thither, he planned to deceive the priest, and so he did, ere they parted; he could not leave off till he had flayed him. It wearieth me when I speak of him; I would fain avenge me on his falsehood, if I wist how; but he goeth hither and thither; he is so fickle he abideth nowhere.

But now, sirs, take heed, for God's love! He took this coal of which I spake, and bare it privily in his hand; and whilst the priest was piling the coals busily, as I told you before, this canon said: "Friend, ye do amiss; this is not piled as it ought to be; but I shall soon amend it. Let me meddle therewith now for a time, for by Saint Gyle! I have pity of you, ye be hot, I see right well how ye sweat. Have this cloth here, and wipe your brow." And while the priest wiped his face, this canon— a curse on him!—took his coal, and laid it above the middle of the crucible, and blew well afterward, till the coals gan burn brightly.

"Now give us drink," quoth he then. "Straightway I undertake all shall be well. Sit we down and let us be merry." And when the canon's beechen coal was burned, anon all the filings fell out of the hollow down into the crucible, as by reason it needs must do, sith it was placed so even above; but alas! thereof wist the priest nothing. He deemed all the coals were alike good, for he comprehended naught of the sleight. And when this alchemist saw his time, "Rise up, sir priest," quoth he, "stand by me; and because I wot well ye have no mould, go walk forth and bring a chalk-stone; for if I may have luck, I will shape one as a mould; and bring with you eke a bowl, or a pan, full of water, and then ye shall see well how our business shall thrive and succeed. And yet, that ye may have no misbelief or wrong conceit of me in your absence, I will not be out of your sight, but go with you, and come back with you." To speak briefly, they opened and shut the chamber-door, and went their way, and carried the key forth with them, and came again without tarrying. Why should I dwell on it all the day long? He took the chalk and wrought it in the shape of a mould, as I shall describe unto you. I say he took out of his own sleeve (evil be his end!) a thin plate of silver, which was but an ounce in weight; and take heed of his cursed trick now! He shaped his mould, in length and breadth, like this plate, so slyly that the priest saw it not; and again he gan hide it in his sleeve; and from the fire he took up his metal, and with merry cheer poured it into the mould; and when he list, he cast it into the water-vessel and straightway bade the priest, "Look what is there, put thy hand in and feel; thou shalt find silver there as I hope." What, devil of hell! should it be else? Silver shavings be silver, pardee! This priest put in his hand and took up a thin plate of fine silver, and glad in every vein was he when he saw that it was so. "God's blessing, and eke his mother's, and all the saints, may ye have, sir canon," said he, "if ye will vouchsafe to teach me this noble craft and subtlety, and I their malison, unless I will be yours, in all things that ever I may."

Quoth the canon: "I will try yet a second time, that ye may observe and be expert in this, and another time at your need essay this process and this crafty art in mine absence. Let us take another ounce of quicksilver, without more words, and do therewith as ye have done erst with that other, which now is silver."

This priest busieth him in all he may to do as this cursed

canon commanded him, and blew the coals hard for to come at his desire. And in the meantime the canon was all ready again to beguile the priest, and for a ruse he bore in his hand an hollow stick (take heed and beware!), in the end of which was put an even ounce of silver filings (as before was put in the coal), and the hollow stopped well with wax, to keep in his filings every whit. And while the priest was busy, this canon with his stick came up anon, and cast in his powder, as he did before (the devil flay him out of his skin, I pray to God, for his falsehood; for he was false ever in thought and deed); and with this stick that was provided with that false contrivance he stirred the coals above the crucible, till the wax melted against the fire, as every man but a fool wot well it needs must do, and all that was in the stick ran out and slipped straightway into the crucible. Now, good sirs, what would ye better than well? When this priest was beguiled again thus, supposing naught but truth, he was so glad that I can express in no manner his mirth and his joy; and thereupon he proffered to the canon both his body and his goods. "Yea," quoth the canon, "though I be poor, thou shalt find me skillful; I warn thee there is yet more to come. Is there any copper here in your house?" "Yea, sir," quoth the priest, "I trow well there be." "Else go buy us some and that straightway. Go forth thy way now, good sir, and hie thee."

He went his way and came with the copper, and the canon took it in his hands, and weighed out of that copper but an ounce. My tongue, as minister of my wit, is all too simple to express the doubleness of this canon, root of all treachery. He seemed friendly to them that knew him not, but he was fiendly both in heart and in mind. It wearieth me to tell of his falseness, yet natheless will I tell of it, to the intent that men may beware thereby, and truly for no other cause.

He put his ounce of copper in the crucible and straightway set it on the fire, and cast powder in, and made the priest to blow and in his working to stoop, as he did before, and all was but a knavish trick; as he list, he made the priest his ape. And afterward he cast it into the mould, and put it at last in the pan of water; and he put in his own hand. And in his sleeve (as ye heard me tell before) he had a thin plate of silver. The cursed hind, slyly he took it out—the priest knowing naught of his false cunning—and in the pan's bottom he left it, and fumbled to and fro in the water, and took up wondrous privily the copper plate and hid it; and caught him by the breast, and spake to him and said thus in his sporting, "Stoop adown, by the mass, ye be to blame; help me now as I did you a while ago. Put in your hand and look what is there." The priest took up anon his plate of silver, and then said the canon, "Let us go with these three plates which we have wrought to some goldsmith, and know if they be worth somewhat; for I would not by my faith, for mine hood, that they were other than pure and fine silver, and that shall straightway be proved."

Unto the goldsmith they went with these three plates and put them to the test with fire and hammer; no man might say but they were as they ought to be.

Who was happier than this besotted priest? Never nightingale joyed better to sing in the season of May, never was bird gladder of the morn, nor ever had lady more delight to carol or to speak of love and womanhood, nor knight to do an hardy deed in arms to stand in the grace of his lady dear, than had this priest to gain knowledge of this sorry craft; and thus he spake to the canon and said, "For love of God that died for us all, and as I may deserve this favour of you, what should this receipt cost? tell now!" "By our lady," quoth this canon, "I warn you well it is dear; for save me and a friar, there can no man make it in England." "No matter," quoth he, "now, sir, for God's sake, what shall I pay? tell me, I prithee." "In sooth," quoth he, "it is full dear. In one word, sir, if ye list to have it, ye shall pay forty pound, so God help me! And were it not for the friendship ye have shown me ere this, ye should pay more, in faith."

This priest fetched anon the sum of forty pound in nobles, and handed them all to this canon for that receipt; yet all its working was but fraud and falsehood.

"Sir priest," he said, "I reck not for renown in my craft, for I would it were kept close; as ye love me, keep it secret; for if men knew all my subtle cunning, they would be so envious of me, by the mass, because of my philosophy, that I should die for it; there were none other end." "God forbid!" quoth the priest, "what say ye? I were mad but I would liefer spend all the goods which I have, than that ye should fall into such misfortune." "Have here right good speed, sir, for your good will," quoth the canon, "grammercy and farewell!" He went his way and never the priest saw him after that hour; and when at such time as he would, the priest came to make essay of this receipt, farewell, then! It would not work. Lo! thus was he duped and beguiled! Thus maketh this canon his first step to bring folk to their destruction.

Consider, sirs, how in every estate of life there is such conflict betwixt men and gold that there is scarce any gold left. This multiplying blindeth so many that in good faith I trow that it is the greatest cause of such scarceness. Philosophers speak so mistily in this craft that men cannot come at their meaning by any wit that men have now. They may well chatter as these jays do, and busily devise strange terms and take delight therein, but they shall never attain to their purpose. If a man have aught, he may lightly learn to multiply and bring his goods to nothing. Lo! in this lusty game is such lucre that it will turn a man's mirth unto bitterness, and empty eke great and heavy purses, and make folk to earn maledictions of them that have lent their goods thereto. Fie! for shame! they that have been burned, alas! cannot they flee the fire's heat? Ye that practise it, I warn you leave it, lest ye lose all; for better is late than never. Never to thrive were too long a date. Though ye prowl for aye, ye shall never discover it. Ye be as bold as Bayard, the blind, that blundereth forth and thinketh no peril; he is ever as bold to run against a stone as to walk aside in the road. So fare ye that multiply, I say. If your eyes cannot see aright, look that your mind lack not its vision. For though ye look never so far abroad and stare, ye shall not win a mite on that business, but waste all ye can clutch and touch. Take the fire away, lest it burn too hard. Meddle no more, I mean, with that art, for if ye do, your thrift is gone utterly. And now will I tell you what philosophers say of this matter.

Lo! Arnold of the New Town saith thus, as his Rosarie maketh mention: "No man can mortify Mercury, unless it be with his brother's knowledge. He that first said this thing was Hermes, father of philosophers; he saith how without doubt the dragon dieth not, unless he be slain by his brother; that is to say by the dragon he understood Mercury and none else; and brimstone by the brother; that were both drawn out of *sol* and *luna*. And therefore," he said, "give heed to my saying: let no man busy him to seek after this art, unless he can understand the intent and speech of philosophers; for if he do, he is an ignorant man. For this science and this cunning, pardee, is of the secret of secrets."

Also there was a disciple of Plato, that on a time asked of his master, as his book Senior will bear witness, "Tell me the name of the secret stone." And Plato answered unto him, "Take the stone that men call Titanos." "Which is that?" quoth he. "The same is magnesia," said Plato. "Yea, sir; is it so? This is *ignotum per ignotius*. Good sir, what is magnesia, I pray you?" "It is a water," quoth Plato, "that is made of four elements." "Tell me, good sir," quoth he then, "the source of that water, if it please you." "Nay, nay," quoth Plato, "that certainly I will not. For all philosophers have sworn that they shall discover it unto none, nor write it in any book, in any manner; for it is so dear unto Christ that he will not that it be discovered, save where it pleaseth his deity to inspire man, and eke he forbiddeth it unto whom it pleaseth him; lo! this is all."

I conclude then thus: Sith God of heaven willeth not that the philosophers declare how a man shall come unto this stone, I counsel, as for the best, to let it go. For whoso maketh God his adversary, as for to work anything in defiance of his will, shall never prosper, though he multiply all his life. And here an end; for my story is done. God send every true man help out of his trouble. Amen.

Here is ended the Canon's Yeoman's Tale.

Notes

The Prologue.

11 *Austin:* i.e. Saint Augustine.

11 *Limiter:* A friar who was assigned certain limits within which to beg.

12 *In principio:* The first words in Latin of the text, "In the beginning was the Word."

12 *Love-days:* Days on which the clergy undertook to settle disputes. The fact that this flattering friar excelled on such occasions suggests that the institution was not very equitable.

13 *Middleburgh and Orwell:* Between about 1384 and 1388 these ports, the one in Holland and the other in Suffolk, were the *termini* of the wool trade. Contemporary documents show that it was often in danger from national enemies and pirates (like the Shipman in the Prologue).

13 *Philosopher:* Chaucer puns on the appropriation to themselves of the word philosopher by the alchemists, who might be supposed to be well provided with gold, since they claimed the ability to make it. (Cf. "Philosopher's stone.")

13 *Paul's church-porch:* A usual gathering-place for lawyers.

14 *Saint Julian:* Patron saint of hospitality, invoked by travellers in need of lodging.

15 *Sweet cyperus:* Parish suppers were sometimes held on the evens before festivals.

NOTES

15 *By Water:* That is, the Shipman made his captives "walk the plank"; threw them overboard.

16 *Images:* It was believed by necromancers and others that acts performed upon the waxen image of a man would produce upon the man himself effects similar to those upon the image, especially if the astrological conditions were favourable.

16 *Esculapius, etc.:* Real and supposed writers on medicine, some ancient, some mediæval, Greek, Arab, Italian, French.

16 *A cordial:* Drinkable gold (*aurum potabile*) was sought after by the alchemists as a sovereign remedy; hence Chaucer's sarcasm.

18 *Tabard:* A sleeveless frock.

19 *Thumb of gold:* The experienced miller succeeds by testing the quality of the meal. But there seems to have been a proverb, "An honest miller has a golden thumb." Hence the *yet.*

20 *Summoner:* An official who cited sinners before the archdeacon's court, which took especial cognizance of matters relating to sexual morality. The summoners were very corrupt and much hated.

21 *Significavit nobis:* The first words of the writ which inflicted temporal punishment on a man condemned by the church; of that at least the summoner was sure. Chaucer's sceptical irony here is due probably to the influence of Wyclif.

21 *Pardoner:* A seller of indulgences.

21 *Vernicle:* The face of Christ is said to have been miraculously pictured on the napkin of Saint Veronica. This relic is reputed to be preserved in Rome, and a copy of it, often worn ostentatiously, was an indication that the wearer had been on pilgrimage thither.

Knight's Tale.

50 *Rubeus, Puella:* Figures used in the species of divination known as geomancy.

51 *Lucina:* The name of Diana as invoked at child-birth.

58 *Against his nature:* The planet Saturn, with which in the Middle Ages the deity was constantly identified, was supposed to cause discord and misfortune.

61 *Prime of day:* About nine o'clock in the morning.

NOTES

Prologue of the Nun's Priest's Tale.

74 The Knight speaks here to the Monk, who has just finished his tale.

Nun's Priest's Tale.

77 *"My lief is faren in londe":* i.e. "My love is gone away"; presumably a song popular at the time.

85 *Undern:* 9 A.M.

87 *Dan Burnel the Ass:* The story is from a poem by Nigellus Wireker, written in the time of Richard I.

90 *My lord archbishop:* The Archbishop of Canterbury, William Courtenay.

Epilogue of Nun's Priest's Tale.

91 *Brasil:* A wood of bright-red colour, used for dyeing.

Wife of Bath's Prologue.

116 *Bigamy:* The wife refers, of course, to consecutive, not to simultaneous, marriages.

120 *Dunmowe:* A prize of a piece of bacon was given at this village to wedded couples who had lived together a year without quarrelling.

120 *Chough:* The reference is to a well-known mediæval story of a man who set an educated crow (or chough) to watch his wife's conduct. When the wife learned that the crow was aware of her trespass, she plotted successfully and most ingeniously with her maid to destroy the crow's credit with her husband.

128 *Ascendent:* The zodiacal sign just ascending above the horizon at the time of a person's birth. It was considered particularly influential on his later life.

130 *Who painted the lion?* The wife refers here to the fable of the Lion and the Man. The latter tried to prove the superiority of his race to the lion's by referring to pictures in which men are killing lions; to which the lion replied that things would be different if lions could draw.

130 *Exaltation:* The exaltation of a planet is the sign in which it is most powerful.

233

NOTES

131 *Lyma and Lucy:* The classical names of these women are Livia and Lucilia.

Clerk's Tale.

151 *Where is your father?* Out of respect the marquis here addresses Grisildis in the plural.

171 *Chichevache:* According to a piece of mediæval folk-lore, two cows, Bicorne and Chichevache, the first very fat, the second very lean, lived respectively on patient husbands and patient wives. The physical condition of each was caused by the ease or difficulty with which the diet was to be come by.

Franklin's Tale.

193 *Tables:* This game, called in Latin *tabularum ludus,* is the modern backgammon.

201 *Nowel:* i.e. the birthday, or Christmas-day, Old French noël, from Latin *natalem.* "To cry Noël" was to sing a Christmas carol, as was usual on Christmas eve.

201 *Toletan tables:* The astronomical tables, composed by order of Alphonso X., King of Castile, about the middle of the thirteenth century, were called sometimes Tabulæ Toletanæ, from their being adapted to the city of Toledo.

201 *Roots:* For an explanation of all these technical terms of mediæval astronomy, see Skeat's Cant. Tales, Vol. V., p. 394.

202 *Fixed Aries:* The true equinoxial point.

Canon's Yeoman's Prologue.

210 *Canon:* A member of a religious order less strict than the orders of monks and friars.

212 *Multiply:* To make gold and silver by the art of alchemy.

Canon's Yeoman's Tale.

220 *Annualer:* A priest who lived by singing anniversary masses for the dead.

223 *Mortify:* i.e. to make the quick (or, living) silver dead.

NOTES

PAGE

229   *Bayard:*   A common name for a horse.

229   *Arnold of the New Town:*   Arnoldus de Villa Nova was a French alchemist of the thirteenth century.   Chaucer quotes here with mockery a specimen of his mystical jargon.   Hermes Trismegistus was believed to be the originator of alchemy; gold and silver were called respectively *sol* and *luna.*

230   *Ignotum per ignotius:*   i.e. to explain an unknown thing by one still more unknown, which Chaucer contemptuously regards as the practice of the alchemists at large.   It need hardly be said that the anecdote is from a mediæval work, and has nothing to do with the historical Plato.